Praise for *Portrait of a Town*

"In *Portrait of a Town*, Pat Parsons reflects with warm nostalgia on her experiences growing up in a lovely and proud Victorian bayside village on the Eastern Shore of Virginia. Her delightful portrayal of daily life during WWII, and of Cape Charles's struggle to survive the changing times, provide valuable insight into the history of the area."

—John M. Barber, Fellow, American Society of Marine Artists

"Pat Parsons's new book, *Portrait of a Town*, speaks of her youth growing up in the Chesapeake Bay waterfront/railroad town on the Eastern Shore of Virginia. Parsons's straightforward approach to storytelling and marvelous memory capture the very essence of small-town American life during the decades of the 1940s and 50s.

Her tales make the reader long for those wonderful, simple days of youth. Although specific to the town of Cape Charles, her well-written stories will interest those near and far as her life memories are a reminder for many of their own lives growing up in small town America. The book is a read well worth reading!"

—Larry Chowning, author of *Harvesting the Chesapeake: Tools and Traditions; Chesapeake Legacy: Tools and Traditions; Chesapeake Bay Buyboats; Deadrise and Cross-planked; Barcat Skipper: Tales of a Tangier Island Waterman;* and other books on the Chesapeake Bay.

PORTRAIT OF A TOWN

Patricia J. Parsons

Portrait of a Town

Cape Charles, 1940–1960

Patricia Joyce Parsons
Illustrations by Hugh Harris

PLEASANT LIVING
BOOKS

ISBN: 978-0-692-43596-0

Library of Congress Control Number: 2015939920

Printed in the United States

Published by

PLEASANT LIVING
BOOKS
www.pleasantlivingmagazine.com/books

To my precious grandchildren:
Anna, Ben, Sarah, Elizabeth, Emily, Emma, Andrew,
Caroline, and triplets Abbie, Maddie, and Ella

TABLE OF CONTENTS

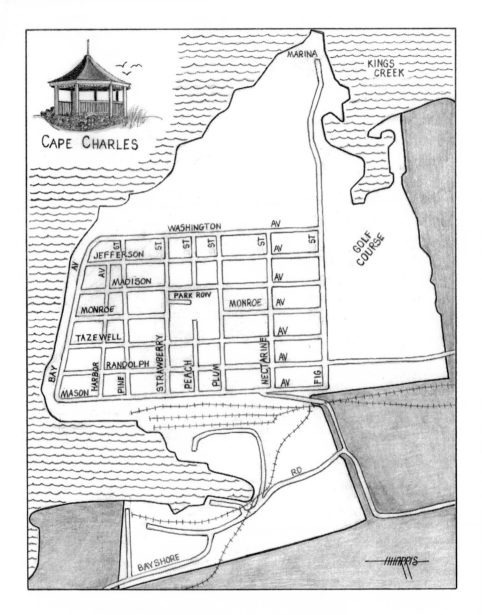

Street map showing Cape Charles's Historic District

Preface

"Don't tell anybody that you come from over here, Mama."

The year was 1975. My ten-year-old daughter and I had just arrived from our home in Richmond and were driving along the beachfront of Cape Charles, Virginia.

Experiencing a surge of nostalgia, I turned away from her. Glancing through the car window toward the horizon of the Chesapeake Bay, I could see part of the beach upon which I had spent so many pleasant hours in my youth. It was now choked with a tangle of sea oats and wiry beach grasses. The boardwalk, where I used to sit to watch the sunsets on summer evenings, was deserted. The benches that once lined the beachfront were gone.

We had turned off the town's main street, with its boarded-up storefronts. Across the street, an empty, unused plot of land gave no indication that at one time, the town's focal point, a bustling railroad/ferry complex, had thrived on that spot. Instead, an unattractive cement factory dominated the view. A few years before, my daughter had been enchanted with the area, but now she was ten, old enough to be embarrassed by the depressing sight of her mother's former hometown.

Here, isolated on the southeastern side of the Chesapeake Bay and surrounded by mile upon mile of farmland, stood a town laid out in an orderly grid that contained many substantial homes. A two-story school; solidly built churches of various denominations; a brick post office, rather large for a small town; and a long main street with two movie theaters, now closed, suggested that in the past this community had enjoyed a vigorous economy. I thought to myself that someone who happened upon this place with no knowledge of its history might ask why a fully formed town such as this sprang up in a place one might describe as "on the edge of nowhere."

Recently, I have returned to find that the community is slowly redefining itself. It now boasts a modest tourist industry, which has resulted in the renovation of a number of the old buildings that line a main street that once again contains shops as well as a couple of nice restaurants. An Irish pub occupies an old bank building. Some of the homes of former residents have been restored and are rented to vacationers who come to Cape Charles to enjoy the sun, the beach, deep-sea fishing, and tours of the wildlife preserve at nearby Kiptopeke. During the 1970s and 1980s, magazine and newspaper articles often referred to Cape Charles as a depressed community, or even as a ghost town. I now hear it called "historic," "charming," or "quaint." Well, I lived in Cape Charles before it was considered charming or quaint, so for those who have just been introduced to Cape Charles and wonder how and why this town existed in such a rural setting, for those who had to move away in order to earn a living, and for those who stayed and care to reminisce, here are a few snapshots of life in Cape Charles before it was "quaint."

Preserving summer's bounty

ABUNDANCE

The Eastern Shore of Virginia lies between the Chesapeake Bay and the Atlantic Ocean, at the southern end of the Delmarva Peninsula, which includes parts of Delaware, Maryland and Virginia. My hometown, Cape Charles, was laid out near the lower part of the peninsula in the late 19th century to accommodate employees of the New York, Philadelphia and Norfolk Railroad, a subsidiary of the Pennsylvania Railroad. It housed the headquarters of the Delmarva Division of the railroad, and before Interstate Route 95 existed, it was considered the gateway to the South. The railroad transported goods and passengers from Philadelphia and points north to Cape Charles, where the railroad's freight cars were loaded onto barges and sent on their way across the Chesapeake Bay to what we on the Eastern Shore called "the mainland." A fleet of ocean-worthy ferries carried the passengers and cars across the Bay.

Extensive railroad shops, a roundhouse, a train station, superintendent's offices, and a ferry terminal formed the focal point of the town's activities. Ferries, tugs, and barges belonged to the railroad, which in later years was simply called the Pennsylvania Railroad. My father was the electrician in charge of the signal system that served the Pennsylvania Railroad's Delmarva Division.

When I was a young child, our country was in the midst of World War II. The railroad was busy moving troops south to the

Cape Charles ferry and on to military installations in the Hampton Roads area and beyond. A nearby army post, Fort John Custis, had been established in 1940, with armed bunkers installed to guard the entrance to the Bay, and lookout towers along the coast manned by soldiers equipped with binoculars. I remember playing on the beach a few miles from town at Pickett's Harbor, under one of the lookout towers.

A short distance away, a prisoner of war camp sat among a grove of pine trees. On Sunday afternoons, following a fulsome midday meal, my father would take the family for a ride up and down the Ocean Highway (Route 13), a two-lane road and the only highway on the Eastern Shore; or along a secondary road called the Seaside Road. As we drove by seemingly endless miles of farmland, we usually passed the prisoner of war camp. From the road, we could see the German prisoners, and though our parents forbade us to stare at the young men behind the wire fences, my sister Jane and I took a good look. How could we resist? The prisoners seemed content, but they must have wondered where in the world they were. I still clearly remember the sight of a young blond German prisoner sitting in the doorway of one of the prison barracks and playing a guitar. He looked so innocent, but of course to us, he was the enemy.

The streets of our town were laid out in a grid, with the east-west streets named for Virginia statesmen and most of the north-south streets named for fruit. Our house on Fig Street had a double lot, and behind it lay eleven acres of fallow fields. During the war, my father rented the field behind the house and set out a Victory Garden, as citizens were encouraged to do. He planted a variety of melons, Golden Bantam corn, lettuce, luscious tomatoes, peppers, and beets that were so good cooked while still small, with their young and tender greens. I had my own crop, a prim row of radishes whose progress I checked daily—although I actually hated radishes, and picked them out whenever they appeared in salads.

Next to the field, a small wilderness lay hidden by honeysuckle vines that hung down in great profusion from an ancient poplar tree. The vines were so old that they had become like rope, and we children loved to swing on them. Pushing aside the vines and undergrowth revealed a long deserted garden containing sweet violets, fennel, asparagus, and various herbs that had been planted by some unknown hand and were now growing wild. How magical it felt to visit our secret garden, chew on pieces of fennel and mint, and inhale the heady perfume of the spring violets.

A huge black walnut tree dominated our backyard. In summer, the black walnuts were covered by fragrant green outer casings. In autumn, they dropped to the ground, and the casings gradually darkened and fell away. The remaining nuts had extremely hard, thick shells. Each November, our mother assigned my younger sister Jane and me the task of shelling the walnuts for the Christmas cakes that she sent to far-off relatives. Seated on the ground, we cracked the nuts between two bricks and laboriously picked out the nut meat. Because the rich taste of the black walnuts was such a treat, it took us a long time to collect enough for the cakes. We usually had to revisit the task for several days.

My father planted flowers on the extra lot next to our house. He never had to fence in his flower or vegetable gardens. We were not bothered with squirrels raiding the vegetables, because those rodents did not exist to any great degree on the southern part of the Eastern Shore. The woods consisted primarily of evergreens, mostly loblolly pine trees that, not producing nuts, did not attract squirrels. Deer did not roam near town, and one rarely saw a rabbit. Since crop-producing fields stretched as far as the eye could see, there was more than enough fodder to satisfy the needs of any hungry wildlife.

With swamps and marshes all around, insects bred freely, so a gardener's prime preoccupation was keeping the bug population from his or her plantings. Japanese beetles loved to dine on our father's roses, so we children were provided with mason jars containing about an inch of kerosene and sent to scoop the beetles into the jars. I hated killing the beetles because I thought they were beautiful, but I realized how important the roses were to Father.

Often, while playing outside, we stopped and helped ourselves to whatever produce caught our fancy. I especially loved to bite into

one of Father's ripe tomatoes, sun-warmed, tangy, sweet, and juicy—
an ideal thirst quencher. Raspberry and blackberry bushes that grew
behind our outbuildings were a mixed attraction because of their
protective thorns. Not so the two enormous fig trees that grew in our
backyard. Their broad branches and felt-like leaves almost reached
the ground, providing a canopy under which Jane and I set up our
"house" or "hideout," depending upon the game of the day. Needless
to say, none of the sweet, soft, sticky figs remained on the lower
branches. We made sure of that.

Because we were allowed to eat any non-poisonous plant that
grew on our own property, Jane and I became, in all innocence, a little
light-fingered with the neighbors' produce. Jane kept two bricks at
the foot of a pecan tree that overhung a nearby alley. Whenever she
felt like having a snack, the brick nutcrackers were always at hand.
In early autumn, we picked big red pomegranates that had ripened
on a bush near the pecan tree. The owners of the pomegranate bush
must have wondered why their ripe fruit disappeared. If they knew,
they never reported it to our parents.

A young couple, Mr. and Mrs. West, originally from Snow Hill,
Maryland, lived in the house next to our vacant lot. There was a barn-
like garage at the back of their yard, around which brightly colored
bantam chickens continually pecked the ground. Every weekend
in the summer, Mr. West made ice cream. He knelt just inside the
doorway of the garage and turned a hand crank that eventually
produced rich frozen custard in the dripping ice-cream maker. Jane
and I were surely a nuisance hanging around the doorway as we
eagerly waited to lick the dasher, which emerged with a thick layer
of frozen goodness adhering to its blades; and which, no doubt, Mr.
West felt he had to offer us.

Along the walls of their garage, the Wests hung strings of onions,
dried herbs, and gourds. Among them, clusters of small peppers of
a vivid, shiny red were suspended from a hook, looking seductively
delicious. Jane and I had often speculated about how they must taste.
One day, Mr. West was working in his garage. When he went back
to his house, he left the door to the garage open. Jane and I moved

quickly as we grabbed some of the luscious-looking peppers. We ran behind the garage and stuffed them into our mouths before our theft could be detected. Aagh! We were immediately, and justly, punished for pilfering those unbearably hot beauties.

In inclement weather, we played in the pantry, a small room off our kitchen. A colorful display of mason jars containing strawberry and peach preserves, stewed figs, red- and green-pepper relish, and tomatoes filled the shelves that lined the perimeter of the pantry. Like all the other ladies up and down "The Shore," my mother canned summer's bounty. Canning season was a frantic time, because no matter what other plans our family might have, fruits and vegetables had to be "put up" when they were ready, not when we were ready. Nature always takes precedence.

Living at the end of a peninsula, with seafood swimming all around us, we enjoyed an abundance of wonderful fresh fish, oysters, clams, and crab. As a picky child, I would not eat seafood of any kind, because I often accompanied my mother to Mr. Crockett's fish shanty, where she made her selection from the morning's catch. The strong smell—or, more accurately, the stench—of old fish drippings made me catch my breath, and gave me a distrust of seafood, so that I missed out on the succulent oysters and freshly caught spot, flounder, and bass that my parents enjoyed. What's more, I equated crabs with poverty. Crabs were so plentiful that the less fortunate could always catch enough to make a meal, as the crab shells scattered around their dwellings so clearly attested. I could not understand why my parents, obviously lacking the insight that I had into the lowly status of the crab, would drive miles up Route 13 to the Shickshinny Restaurant because they considered the crab cakes there such a delicacy.

Early on summer mornings, hucksters wandered the streets, calling out their wares. Fig Street was usually their first stop as they made their sales rounds. When huckleberries were in season, our mother kept her ear alert for the coming of the black vendor who, in a melodious voice, sang, "Huckleberries, huckleberries!" as he pushed his fruit cart down the street. I can still picture Mother running out of the kitchen and down the back porch steps to catch him before someone else could buy up the tiny wild berries, which she maintained had a richer flavor than regular blueberries and which were delicious sprinkled on cereal or baked in pies.

Farmer Long brought his tree-ripened peaches from farther up the county. He sold the big golden fruit by the bushel from the back of a trailer attached to his car, which he parked at a corner near our house. Mother hastened to buy his peaches for canning, but we children always got some for immediate consumption. Unable to wait, Jane and I stood at the curb beside Mr. Long's auto, sweet peach juice running down our chins and staining our pinafores as we bit into the intensely flavorful fruit.

Occasionally, the elderly Mr. Crockett, of fish store renown, came down the street, pushing a wooden handcart loaded with dripping ice and fresh fish. He heralded his approach by blowing his fish horn. It had a slow, mournful, slightly echoing sound; an ancient sound that must have been heard along the Mediterranean Sea at the dawn of Western civilization, as Triton is pictured blowing such a horn in mosaics of antiquity and in old fountains of the Italian Renaissance.

Gladstone's Dairy was located on the part of Fig Street that led to Kings Creek. If you walked or drove toward Kings Creek, you could see Mr. Gladstone's cows calmly grazing in the meadow on the left side of the road. Mr. Gladstone's milk was delivered in glass bottles—and what delicious milk it was. A layer of heavy cream always formed on top of the milk. Sometimes, Mother shook the bottle to incorporate the cream into the rest of the milk; and sometimes the plug of cream that formed at the top of the bottle was so thick, she dislodged it with a knife and set it aside to use as topping for berries or dessert.

In a little neighborhood called Birdsnest, about fifteen miles north of Cape Charles, there lived a woman Father knew who raised chickens. Each week when he made the trip up the county to check the signals along the railroad tracks, Father would stop at her poultry farm. He always bought some of her fresh farm-produced eggs. Jane and I thought it was immensely funny that our eggs came from "a bird's nest," but our father maintained that those were the best eggs one could possibly find. It must have been so, because for years, he continued to buy our eggs in Birdsnest.

Mother often remarked that, unlike the parts of the country that experienced wartime food shortages, we barely knew the deprivations of war, thanks to the eggs, dairy products, and produce that our farming and fishing community so abundantly provided.

Mandy Trower

Although many African-Americans objected to the original picture of Aunt Jemima on her breakfast food advertisements, there really were women who looked like she did before her makeover gave her a slimmed-down, more modern image. Amanda "Mandy" Trower was such a one, and she looked beautiful to me.

Mandy was a large older woman, of dark complexion, with a pleasant round face and tiny pigtails that stuck up all over her head. She helped my mother with the housework, and on wash day, she helped with the laundry. Wash day was a miserable day at our house. The washing machine was pulled out of the pantry and filled with hot water. Dripping clothes were put through a wringer attached to the washing machine, and then dropped from the wringer into a laundry basket or dipped in a homemade starch solution and wrung out again. Next, they were taken into the backyard and hung on several clotheslines that crossed the yard. I always dreaded wash day, because Mother was sure to be in a bad humor. Then there was the mess in the kitchen, and I knew that there would be nothing good for lunch.

On Mondays, all day was dedicated to doing the washing. On Tuesdays, Mandy's niece Laura came to iron the clothes that Mother had sprinkled the night before with water from a Coke bottle fitted with a stopper that looked like a little showerhead. She tightly wrapped them, so that the moisture would evenly dampen the items to be ironed in the morning.

Keeping up with the laundry was important, because our family used a lot of clothes. My father always put on a clean white shirt in the evening after he washed up for dinner. Every day at four o'clock, Mother changed into a fresh dress, and changed us children into fresh clothes, as well. Most of the women in our town did the same. Then, they would sit on their porches on late afternoons in summer and perform light tasks, such as shelling peas or stringing the green beans that we called "snaps," while waiting for their husbands to come home from work. The whistle from the railroad shops blew at five o'clock. It could be heard all over town, and signaled the end of the workday for many of the town's citizens.

One December, after our mother had mailed her famous Christmas fruitcakes to faraway relatives, she went into the pantry to get some flour from the large sack of flour she had purchased to use in the Christmas baking. She opened the sack and cried out with horror. "Oh, Mandy, look! This flour is full of bugs, and I used it for the fruitcakes!" Mandy started to laugh. Her laughter rose slowly from deep within her chest. Then she sat down in the kitchen's rocking chair as her laughter increased. She started to rock back and forth in the rocker, laughing until tears ran down her cheeks. Still laughing, she pulled out the oversized white handkerchief she always kept stuffed in the bosom of her blouse and pressed it to her face. "What is so funny?" Mother asked, perturbed by Mandy's reaction.

"Heh, heh, heh . . ." Mandy's voice pitched higher with laughter. "Oh, Miss Joyce," she said, "just t'ink—whoever eats de mos' fruitcake, gets de mos' bugs."

Sometimes in summer, when our mother needed to get my sister and me out from underfoot, she asked Mandy to take us to the beach, which was several blocks from our home. We trotted along the sidewalk in our bathing suits, towels around our shoulders and sand buckets on our arms. I felt deeply embarrassed to be seen with Mandy because, before we left the house, she changed into bedroom slippers—and even worse, she did not use the sidewalk. Instead she walked on the grass beside us while dipping snuff from the little round container that she always kept with her. I would try to coax her onto the sidewalk, but she said that the hot, hard pavement hurt her feet.

Mother was always happy to see Mandy's face at the door in the morning. She sometimes rushed to tell Mandy how much work there was to do and how overwhelmed she felt. Mandy, ever wise, would say, "Now Miss Joyce, don't you worry. It ain't duh work dat's so bad, it's jus' duh t'inking about it." That became a mantra that the whole family eventually used when facing a daunting task. To this day, I can prod myself into activity by the thought of Mandy saying "It ain't duh work's so bad, it's jus' duh t'inking about it."

Porches

I once heard a real estate guru in Richmond say that he thought the crime rate rose when they stopped building houses with porches. I can understand how that might be true. In Cape Charles, the houses, like most that were built during the late 1800s and early 1900s, had porches. One of the beauties of Cape Charles was the variety of porches that could be seen around town. Every house had one. Some were so deep that, any time of day, they were partly shaded. Some curved around their house like the arm of a protective parent. On others, ornate fretwork lent turn-of-the century charm to the streets.

Residents of Cape Charles sat on their porches during summer afternoons and evenings. From the vantage point of their porch swings and gliders, they could, and did, keep a sharp eye on what was happening in the neighborhood. Why not? After all, a healthy interest in the affairs of others helps to relieve the light air of boredom that can hover over the daily life of a small town.

There was one family in town whose house sat farther back from the street than their neighbors' houses, which afforded them only a narrow view from their porch. This forced the two grown daughters of that household into their car. As they cruised along the streets of the town, all one could see at the passenger-seat window were the two round lenses of a pair of binoculars directed at oneself. These young ladies, who prided themselves on their own proper behavior, showed particular interest in watching the seagulls along the beachfront—which was a popular spot to park and neck. If the binoculars chanced to slip and catch embracing couples within their focus, well, accidents do happen.

Although Cape Charles was surrounded by miles and miles of undeveloped land, many of its houses were built close enough to one another that neighbors could sit on their porch swings and hold a conversation with each other or greet passersby from the front-porch railing.

Some of the townspeople had screened in their front porches in order to keep out the mosquitoes and other flying pests that were so prevalent on the Eastern Shore. This gave them the advantage of being able to observe others while remaining anonymous behind their grey scrim. Still, since many of the porches in Cape Charles were quite beautiful, their owners would not dream of defacing their appearance with screening. Those of us who sat on open porches on warm evenings burned pots of citronella candles to repel the insects. If one took a stroll around town on a summer night, the scent of citronella and the soft murmur of conversation would waft toward him or her from the darkened porches.

For children, the hours between dinner and bedtime were the very best time to play outside. In summer, the neighborhood children congregated on the sidewalk while their parents relaxed on the porches. As darkness fell, lightning bugs flitted and blinked around us as we played noisy games of tag or Red Rover until it was so dark we could hardly see each other. There was a feverish urgency to fill these last hours with the exhilaration of running, shouting, and playing with complete abandon, for we knew that our day would end when our parents called us to come inside to get ready for bed. How we begged to linger out-of-doors for just a few more moments—and how seldom that request was granted.

THE NEW BABY

In January of 1942, Dr. Lynch, our family physician, consoled Mother, who was feeling overwhelmed by the thought of a third pregnancy. He maintained that if she could ride with him on his visits out into the country and see all the lonely elderly people who had no children and no one to look in on them when they were ill, she would feel differently. "Believe me," he told her, "someday you will be glad that you have this child."

White-haired, gentlemanly, Dr. Mortimer Lynch was from a different era, having studied medicine under Dr. Walter Reed. He had served Northampton County as one of its dedicated physicians for many years and was now turning some of his practice over to Dr. S. K. Ames, who had recently opened an office in Cape Charles. He was planning to retire soon. No longer up to making the trip to the nearest hospital in Nassawadox at all times of the night or day to deliver babies, he suggested that Mother engage Dr. Ames to see her through this pregnancy.

That was in January of 1942. On the first of July, when it was obvious that the baby was on its way, Father called Dr. Ames, who soon arrived at our house in his brand-new car, ready to drive Mother to the hospital nineteen miles north of Cape Charles. "Please, hold back. Please, don't have the baby now, not in my new car," Mother recalled him repeating as they sped along Route 13. They made it to the hospital in time; my brother, Jerry, came into the world; and there were no problems with the delivery. The problems began later.

After two weeks in the hospital, Mother arrived home to be greeted by Ella Scott, a practical nurse; and Aunt Margaret, my father's single older sister, who had arrived to help out while Mother was still in the hospital. Ella Scott was a heavyset black woman. She wore a spotless white nurse's uniform, with a shiny gold pin, the emblem of her profession, on her collar. She immediately took charge of the baby, exclaiming, "He's a gold dollah! He sure is a gold dollah." It was her job to take care of Jerry, and she made it clear that that was the only thing she could be expected to do.

Aunt Margaret focused her energies on seeing to the comfort of her brother. After all, being much older than he, she had helped to raise him, and this gave them a special bond. Mandy continued to come on cleaning day and laundry day. That left Mother to provide meals for the family and for those who had come to help, to take care of Jane and me, and to see to the other household needs.

My father was now fifty-five years old, and he was sensitive about the fact that his children were so young. On the Eastern Shore, where early marriages were the norm, Mother's age of thirty-eight and Father's of fifty-five made them older parents indeed.

At that time, wartime food rationing was in force. With so many people in the house, the food supplies dwindled quickly. Father made frequent trips to pick up a few extra groceries at Pender's store on Mason Avenue, and I was allowed to tag along. Pender's was a grocery chain out of Norfolk, and some of the clerks, not being from Cape Charles, did not know Father. They officiously questioned his entitlement to purchase the amount of milk and other rationed items that a family with three young children needed. Father's face flushed with indignation at being accused of defrauding the rationing board as if he were a thief, while I blushed with embarrassment. If there were other customers in the store who knew Father, they would step up to verify that he did indeed have a young family.

With Mother busy with baby matters, Father relieved the household congestion by taking Jane and me for walks whenever he could. Our walks usually took us to the beachfront. As it was summer,

Jane and I headed straight into the water, which was shallow for quite a way out, providing a large sandbar on which young children could safely play. We busily collected treasures that had accumulated along the shore: seaweed of different types, sea-etched pieces of glass, a variety of small shells, bits of straw and tar and bleached driftwood, all waiting to be picked up by delighted children.

As we walked along the boardwalk, we might be approached by Gussie, one of the town's more colorful characters. A little wizened figure in an odd assortment of clothes, she could be seen roaming the streets, stopping from time to time to rummage through the garbage cans. If she found something that she deemed useful, she deposited it in the large bag that she always carried. "I see you got you gran'chill'en today," she unfailingly remarked as she greeted Father with a toothless grin. Although visibly annoyed by her suggestion that he might be our grandfather, he managed to give her a small donation and appeared relieved when she moved on down the street.

Several times that summer, when we were at the beach, a sudden squall appeared on the horizon. As the moving curtain of rain roiled toward land, we would grab our towels and other beach accoutrements and make a frenzied dash toward home. If we were caught by the rain, the plump raindrops hitting the hot sidewalk sent out a steamy ozone smell as lightning crackled all around us. How delightfully terrifying it was!

We returned home to the fuss of baby bottles being sterilized and baby being bathed, fed and placed in a window under mosquito netting for his "sun bath" as Dr. Ames had ordered. Mother would be busy preparing dinner, while Aunt Margaret encouraged her brother to take a rest before supper. When dinnertime came, Aunt Margaret was quick to see that Father was served. Then, before everyone had finished eating, she would jump up to bring Father his coffee and dessert, much to Mother's annoyance.

A few weeks after Jerry's birth, Ella Scott left to care for another newborn, leaving Mother full care of the baby. Then, though her first concern remained her brother's welfare, Aunt Margaret offered to do some of the baking. She did not cook, but she was a talented baker. Her piecrusts were always flaky, her cakes light and moist, and her dinner rolls came to the table with a fragrant, yeasty aroma. Mother appreciated the delicious baked items that Aunt Margaret contributed to the evening meals and often told her so, but Aunt Margaret never commented on the meals Mother prepared.

At one Friday evening's dinner, Mother passed Aunt Margaret a platter of plump, freshly shucked oysters that had been rolled in batter, then in bread crumbs, and fried just long enough to have a crispy, light brown coating. Margaret passed the platter on to Father. "I don't like oysters," she proclaimed.

Father set the platter on the table in front of Aunt Margaret and looked at his sister with a steely blue stare. "You'll like these oysters." At the sharp edge to his voice, all around the table fell silent, surprised that he was taking an assertive tone with his older sister.

Aunt Margaret picked up the serving fork and added two oysters to her plate. She gingerly lifted her fork to her lips and took a bite.

"These are delicious," she pronounced, as if greatly surprised. Mother flushed with pleasure.

A month later, Father saw Aunt Margaret off at the train station. Jane and I knew we would miss her and the little presents that she occasionally slipped to us, gifts that Mother complained were aimed at "trying to wean my children away from me." But now, with the last of her helpers gone, Mother finally had her husband, her daughters, and her baby to herself—and many times over the years, she retold the story of the oysters and the night that her husband championed her against his powerful sister.

Liquid Refreshment

Sometimes, when out for a walk, Mother stopped to make a purchase at Savage & Blasingame's, later called Savage's Drug Store, located at the corner of Mason Avenue and Strawberry Street. When we were small, it had marble counters, dainty wrought-iron chairs with round seats, and glass-topped tables. This lent it the charm of a late nineteenth-century pharmacy. Once we set foot inside Savage's, Jane and I knew that we would be treated to small dishes of ice cream.

As we got older, we preferred one of Savage's thick, creamy milkshakes. But Savage's was known for other drinks, as it was widely acknowledged that the group of men who met in the back room of Savage's on Sundays after church gathered there to treat their coughs and other complaints with a few medicinal highballs. Virginia was a dry state with Blue Laws that required businesses to be closed on Sundays and prohibited the sale of liquor by the glass at any time. Drugstores, however, could open for a few hours on Sundays, and pharmacists were permitted to keep a supply of alcoholic beverages on hand for use in preparing tonics, cough syrups, and other remedies. So, what law could prevent Mr. Savage from hosting his friends to a fortifying drink on an early Sunday afternoon?

Liquor had to be purchased from the state-controlled ABC store further down the street on Mason Avenue. Of course, my mother, as a respectable woman, would never be seen entering the ABC store. If she needed brandy for the fruitcakes she made for Christmas or spirits for other culinary reasons, she walked over to Front Street, as Mason Avenue was often called, and approached any man she saw loitering nearby who looked as if he could use some money. She gave him the money to purchase the required alcoholic beverage and waited outside the ABC store for her surrogate to emerge and pass her the precious package. Then she slipped him his tip and hurried off down the street.

Mother had another provider of spirits. Belle Bilich ran a small grocery store on Mason Avenue. Belle carried a line of kosher goods, which meant that she was permitted to sell Manischewitz wine. She was a friendly woman with dark brown hair and lively brown eyes. Mother often spoke of how much she admired Mrs. Bilich, both for her industry and the accommodating manner she showed toward her customers. She liked Belle personally, but she also liked the fact that, if she wanted wine for any reason, Mrs. Bilich would discreetly tuck a bottle or two of Manischewitz in with our family's grocery order.

The adults were not the only ones with a clandestine source of drinking materials. In the first block of Mason Avenue west of Fig Street, Jeff's, a black-owned store, and Ewell's, which belonged to a white owner, were housed in two of the oldest buildings in town. In fact, the floors at Jeff's were so old that they were black with age. Both were typical old-fashioned grocery stores, where the grocer stood behind the counter to wait on customers.

Occasionally in summer, we children were given a few coins and permission to walk over to Mason Avenue to buy ice cream. We happily set out with other children from the neighborhood for this rare adventure. Mother forbade us to go to Jeff's, but gave us permission to walk farther down the street to Ewell's. Sometimes, however, we chose to patronize Jeff's. Jeff's store seemed dark as a cave as we came in out of the summer sunshine. A group of elderly black men, seated on chairs and crates within range of the breeze from the large floor fan, chatted about events in Jersey, the part of town in which they lived. As we trooped across the doorway and made our way toward the drinks cooler, the men's conversation ceased. With only the sound of the fan whirring softly in the background, we plunged our arms up to the elbows into the wonderfully wet chunks of ice in the big sweating cooler and fished up a grape soda or a Big Orange. We opened the bottles with the bottle opener attached to the side of the cooler, paid the grocer, and rushed back into the street to drink up our "grapes" and "Big Oranges" before going home, because we had been permitted to buy ice cream, not drinks.

Soft drinks, except for homemade root beer and an occasional ginger ale, were seldom served at our house, as Mother maintained that drinking soft drinks in youth would lead to consuming hard liquor later in life. What's more, we were never allowed to drink a soft drink from a bottle, only from a glass—so we were being doubly disobedient at Jeff's. We soon learned to avoid buying the grape drinks. Purple lips and tongues always gave us away when we returned home. Years later, when we admitted that we used to buy treats at Jeff's, Mother confessed that her objection to our appearing at Jeff's was not that we were in any danger there, but because she felt that the unusual presence of a group of white children might seem invasive to some of Jeff's other customers.

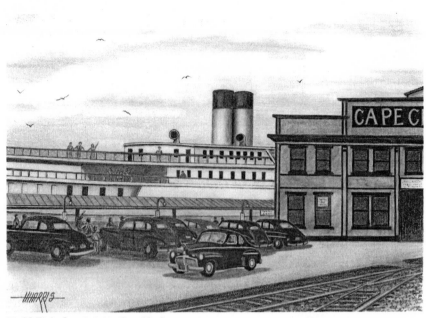
The SS Elisha Lee *docked in Cape Charles*

CROSSING THE BAY DURING WORLD WAR II

The predawn fog was starting to lift. From the deck of the *SS Elisha Lee*, we could see Father below us on the dock where we had waited in the early morning chill for the gangplank of the Cape Charles ferry to be lowered. He had driven Mother, my sister Jane, and me the few blocks from our home to meet one of the seven big ocean-worthy ferries that linked Cape Charles to the mainland.

The year was 1944. I was eight years old, and Jane was six. We were making one of our infrequent trips to Norfolk to buy clothes for the coming autumn, and here we were on deck, dressed as if we were going to church. All around us, sailors in white uniforms settled in the deck chairs like a flock of alighting seagulls, or paced the deck, relieved to be stretching their legs. They had come on the overnight train from Philadelphia and beyond to be deployed at the Norfolk

Naval Base, or aboard one of the warships anchored in Hampton Roads.

Along the street facing the Bay, a line of exhausted travelers, many of whom had driven a hundred and seventy miles down a peninsula with unvarying rural scenery, waited impatiently to steer their cars into the gaping mouth of the ferry. The agitated complaints of those who were standing in the street beside their cars drifted up to us. One could sense the anxiety of others near the end of the queue, who feared that they might have to wait an hour longer for the next ferry if there was no more room on board.

When the cars were finally loaded and the bustle of releasing the ferry from its moorings had ceased, we went inside for cocoa and doughnuts that Mother purchased from the white-coated waiter. After we finished our cocoa, we hurried back out on deck to watch the sunrise as our small hometown of Cape Charles dropped from view and we found ourselves completely out of sight of land. We soon came back inside, where Mother sat trying to scan the *Norfolk Ledger-Dispatch* while keeping a sharp eye on our movements. A few minutes later we wanted to be outside again—and so it went: inside, then out. With nothing to look at except endless water and the seagulls that were following the ferry, we soon got bored—until, much to our delight, the grey humps of several porpoises broke the surface and then slipped beneath the waves. Jane and I stood at the rail as we peered across the water, but our hopes of seeing another vigorous display from the porpoises ended in disappointment.

After what seemed like a very long time, a strip of land appeared. We were approaching Old Point Comfort, always a familiar stop on our three-hour trip to Norfolk. "Now," I thought, "at last, we are out in the world, where big things are happening." We pulled up in front of the massive red-brick Chamberlain Hotel, located on the grounds of Fort Monroe. Gazing at the hotel across the railing of the *Elisha Lee*, I felt that I was looking at a castle. Mother, standing beside us, told us that the government had commandeered the hotel for wartime use by the military, and indeed, it presented a grand air of "spit and polish," with flags flying, and planters of flowers, tables, chairs, and colorful umbrellas in place around the pool. Lined up with military precision near the hotel, a row of identical red-brick houses with white front porches faced the harbor. These, Mother explained, housed high military officials. It all seemed so wonderful.

"Why don't we get off the ferry, Mama, and go inside the hotel? We can catch another boat to Norfolk."

Mother didn't have to say "no" of her own volition. She had the handy excuse that the Chamberlain was off-limits to all but the military.

We left the pageantry of Old Point Comfort, with its holiday-like ambiance. As the *Elisha Lee* pushed its way toward Norfolk, Mother reverently named the large ships that we passed: "This is the battleship *Missouri*." Or, "Look! There's the cruiser *Alaska*." Battleships, aircraft carriers, and destroyers crammed the harbor, along with smaller escorts and tenders. All this weighty evidence of war was sobering and left me feeling anxious, partly because our parents hadn't spared us any of the details about the conflicts in Europe and Asia, and partly because Mother became visibly uneasy when, as we approached the Naval Base, people of Asian appearance, speaking a language we didn't understand, excitedly rushed to the rail, clicking their cameras for all they were worth.

When the ferry finally docked, we walked a block or two over to Granby Street and the department stores. The streets in downtown Norfolk were jammed shoulder to shoulder with jostling pedestrians, mostly sailors. Gasoline fumes from the congestion of buses and cars seemed to hang above the scorching pavement. Mother held our hands tightly as we made our way into the fray.

Our first stop was Hofheimer's Shoe Store, which contained something wondrous: an X-ray machine, into which you could slide your foot and, peering through a viewer, actually see its bones within the outline of your shoe. Unaware of the danger of overexposure to X-rays, we children took turns pushing each other aside so we could look into the machine.

During the war, although leather goods were rationed and scarce, Hofheimer's had a decent supply of shoes. Mother was delighted to be able to purchase two pairs of Buster Brown oxfords. She handed the salesman her shoe ration coupons and paid for the shoes, and we headed once again into the crowded and noisy street.

The only department stores in Norfolk that Mother would patronize were Ames & Brownley and Smith & Welton, stores that she said carried the best-quality goods. How tired and bored I became while Mother tried plaid fall dresses and school clothes on Jane and me, first at Smith & Welton and then at Ames & Brownley. I shifted impatiently from foot to foot while I waited for Jane to try on clothes, until it was my turn.

Lunch at Smith & Welton was a must when we came to Norfolk, so we hurried back and took the elevator up to the tearoom. The nicely set tables and soft tinkle of glassware and silver provided an atmosphere of gentility after the bustle of the street. Murals with nautical themes surrounded the restaurant space. Jane and I ordered the flavorful pimento cheese sandwiches for which the tearoom was known, and Mother had chicken salad. We sipped small bowls of soup and, later, dug into scoops of ice cream that were beautifully served in little silvery cups with lace paper doilies underneath. Mother complained that it was impossible to get a good cup of tea in Norfolk because the drinking water tasted so much like chlorine.

After lunch, Mother, who had not yet made purchases from either store, took us down to the children's department at Smith & Welton, where she bought a few items. Then we walked back to Ames & Brownley for the things that she liked better there. One of the salesladies remarked that the people from the Eastern Shore were rich. That made me feel very grand, but Mother informed her that because the Eastern Shore people only got to the mainland a few times a year, they had to make purchases for an entire season in one trip, which made us look as if we had large amounts of money to spend. By the end of the day we were feeling pretty grumpy as, laden with packages, we dragged ourselves back to the dock.

It was dark when we pulled away from Norfolk and entered the Chesapeake Bay. The long white beam of a searchlight moved back and forth across the sky. Reflected lights from waterside communities shimmered in the water along the shoreline of Hampton Roads. Once we moved out of sight of the mainland, all became black, except for the faint glow from a ship off in the distance and an occasional channel marker. We continued through the silent waters until we reached Cape Charles, to be greeted with the sound of fog horns in the harbor; Father; and, at last, our beds.

The Gorilla

School

In September of 1942, at age six, I became a student at Cape Charles High School. It was the only school in Cape Charles, and it provided a good education to pupils from the first grade through high school graduation. One was often teased for being a seven-, eight-, or ten-year-old attending high school and, while the joke became rather worn, the small school operated like a good family, with teachers as parents, and children of all ages under one roof.

I will never forget my first day of school. Like all the children who lived in town, I walked to school. Clutching a notebook and pencil box and dressed in an autumnal plaid frock of crisp cotton, I walked to the end of our block of Fig Street. I turned the corner onto Tazewell Avenue and, approaching the house of a merchant mariner, I heard a sound like a groan, accompanied by the clatter of wood hitting wood. I turned my head quickly toward the noise.

There, on the vacant lot next to the mariner's house, stood a cage about the size of an average toolshed—and inside the cage, looking straight at me, was an enormous gorilla that the mariner had brought back from one of his voyages. His huge hairy hands were shaking his cage so violently that I could picture it breaking apart and the gorilla, released from his imprisonment, chasing me down the street.

Heart pounding, I started to run away, but the sound of the rattling cage followed me. Just then, Mr. Lawson, the school principal who boarded in the house across from the gorilla, came out. Since an older child from the neighborhood had previously told me that Mr. Lawson was the school's dispenser of punishments, I was leery of him, too. He was, however, preferable to the gorilla, so I quickly fell into step with him.

Mr. Lawson asked if this was my first day of school. His questions and comments were reassuring, and it was a comfort to know that no big animal dared mess with me while I was under the protection of such an influential man.

The fragrance of cedar from the sawdust and oil with which the floors were cleaned made the school smell like a newly sharpened pencil. The students, many in new clothes and new shoes, and clutching new notebooks filled with fresh new paper, crowded the hallway. The first-graders were met by our teacher, Miss Becky Scott. She directed us to our classroom.

Miss Scott was a strict, grey-haired lady who adhered to an old style of teaching that tolerated no nonsense. First she showed us the cloakroom at the back of the class. There we could store extra books, lunch boxes, and pencil cases, and hang up our coats once the weather turned cold. She informed us that children who dared to talk out of turn or cause a disturbance would be sent to sit all alone in the cloakroom.

After checking to make sure that we all knew our ABC's, Miss Scott passed out our reader, *Fun with Dick and Jane*, and helped us sound out the first few words. Then she set about correcting the way we held our pencils. Since I had poor fine motor skills, I received some painful raps on the knuckles from her ruler for my fumbling attempts to hold my pencil to her satisfaction. I soon found an excuse to escape to the girls' bathroom.

As I was washing my hands, I looked up into the plate glass mirror behind the sink to see a tall girl, about eleven years of age, looking into the mirror as she slowly and repetitiously combed her dark shiny hair. When she noticed me, Peggy Jane turned on me and, to my horror, spat out, "What are you staring at, you dumb-looking kid!" Then to my relief, the bell announcing the end of the first day of school rang out.

After that first day, things did get better. The gorilla was not always in the yard, and when he was there, I would hang back before passing the merchant mariner's house, and wait for Mr. Lawson to appear. I eventually discovered that an alley between Tazewell and Monroe Avenues completely bypassed the gorilla house and led straight to the school grounds. Miss Scott turned out to be an excellent teacher, and kind in her own stern way. I never had to sit in the cloakroom, but my sister Jane, who was very talkative, found herself there often. She told me that she didn't mind because, while there, she could rifle through the pockets of the other children and treat herself to any candy she found. Fortunately, I had no more unkind words from Peggy Jane who, like me, was only dawdling in the girls' room while waiting for the dismissal bell to ring.

The school issued each of us a little book called *My Victory Book* to be filled with stamps that were sold at school for ten cents apiece. When stamps had been pasted into all the spaces provided, the book could be turned in at the post office for a twenty-five-dollar war bond. This was money we children loaned the government for the war effort. We also were given cards with tight slots, into which we painstakingly inserted dimes. We were asked to canvas the community, begging dimes from our neighbors. At the end of each week, the school collected our dimes and sent them to the March of Dimes Foundation that had been established to combat polio, a scourge that was greatly feared by parents everywhere.

Students who lived in town walked home for lunch. Those who lived in the county, and whose parents paid tuition for them to attend Cape Charles High School, brought their lunches in brown paper bags after they became too old to carry such a childish item as a lunchbox. I often wished that I could bring my lunch in a brown bag like the county children and sit at my desk or out on the school grounds at lunchtime with the other "brown baggers." But my mother thought it was important that her children come home for a hot lunch.

Sometimes, on the way back to school after lunch, we stopped at the home of Mrs. Baker on Monroe Avenue. Mrs. Baker's husband was often away for long periods with the Merchant Marine. In his absence, she stayed with her daughter and spent her time working on crafts and making cakes and other items that she sold. Mrs. Baker was a heavyset woman whose red-cheeked face reminded me of an apple. That was interesting, because in the fall when apples were in season, she made candy apples that she sold to the schoolchildren during our lunch breaks. She always let it be known ahead of time which days she would have the candy apples ready. Then children gathered on her front porch and rang her doorbell until she appeared bearing a large tray of apples, each impaled on a stick and sitting in a little puddle of its thick coating of caramel, chocolate, or cinnamon. Her candy apples were unforgettably delicious, but the teachers did not appreciate our returning to class with sticky hands and faces, and with sticky half-eaten apples that had to be stored somewhere for the rest of the afternoon. Whenever I could, I snuck my apple into the little shelf under my desk and surreptitiously took a bite when the teacher's back was turned. If she caught me red-handed, she would confiscate the forbidden fruit. Some teachers put confiscated apples aside on a piece of paper and returned them after school, but others grabbed the gooey treasures away and threw them into the wastepaper basket.

Another source of treats was the candy counter of Raynes' Grocery Store, located near the school on Plum Street. At lunchtime and recess, children crowded around the candy counter, trying to decide which candies would give them the most pieces for a nickel, while Mr. Rayne stood patiently by. Among my favorites were little wax bottles that contained a sweet liquid of green, orange, red, or purple. We could bite the tops off to access the nectar within. Then there were the bright red wax lips that stuck out when I slid them onto my mouth. When I became tired of goofing around, trying to be funny with my big protruding lips, I could break them up and chew the wax to extract the sugar.

In autumn, I often arrived at school bearing a huge bouquet of freshly cut dahlias to decorate my teacher's desk. Father had good success with the dahlias that he grew in a big square plot at the edge of our yard. Some of them were a deep burgundy, some a golden rust shade, and there was a wide spectrum of rich colors in between. The flowers, some as large as my head, stood ramrod-straight on their stems as I carried them to school. The teacher placed the dahlias into a vase, and when she set them on the edge of her desk, their brilliance seemed to fill the room with color. I hope she realized that they were sent as a token of appreciation for all her efforts, for as my mother often said, "One of the most generous things a person can do in this life is to pass his or her knowledge on to another."

Evidence of War

One day, as Mother and I walked from Fig Street toward the beach, we passed the home of the McMath family, owners of one of the pharmacies in Cape Charles. A small white banner bearing an embroidered gold star was hanging in their living room window. Mother told me that it was placed there to memorialize the son they had recently lost when, as a prisoner of the Japanese, his prison ship was torpedoed and sank. We continued on our way. Mother pointed out similar banners in the windows of many of the other houses. Each banner was of white silk, with an embroidered star at its center. A blue star indicated that someone from that household was actively serving in the military, and a gold star commemorated a serviceman who had perished in the war. As we passed the homes displaying banners, Mother breathed a prayer for those parents and their sons and daughters in uniform.

World War II seemed very close. Because we lived at the edge of the Chesapeake Bay near the Atlantic Ocean, I imagined that London, like Norfolk, lay just beyond the horizon. War news was fully reported over the radio, and at our house, the kitchen radio played all day long, so we were fed a constant stream of combat information.

The war was vividly portrayed by the *News of the World*, which I saw each week at the movies. No matter that a movie appropriate for a child was the featured film; we children cringed through the

RKO Movietone News scenes depicting the London Blitz, bombs descending on already-burning European cities, strafed airplanes falling from the sky, or torpedoed warships sinking in the Pacific Ocean, their sailors still on board.

Out in the reassuring light of day, we children bravely chased imaginary Tojos and Hirohitos down the street. We ridiculed Hitler by placing our fingers under our noses to replicate his moustache and, extending our arms in stiff salute, we called out, "Hi-Ho Hitler."

The daily comings and goings of military convoys that rumbled along Route 13 and the sight of battleships, aircraft carriers, amphibious vessels, and tenders crowding the harbor every time we took the ferry to Norfolk were reminders that we were a country at war. In addition, tales of German submarines being sighted off the Virginia Capes—Cape Henry in the south, and our own Cape Charles—flew through our community. Our father, a civilian who had served in the army's signal corps during the First World War, was sometimes called to the Navy Yard in Norfolk. He never divulged what he was doing there. "Loose lips sink ships" was the motto of the day.

Air raid drills were intended to accustom the population to darken the coastline in case of a nocturnal aerial attack by the enemy. To me, the periodic air raid drills were frightening, but at the same time, they provided an exciting change in our normal routine. These blackouts, as they were called, brought the war straight into our house. Whenever intermittent blasts from the volunteer fire department's siren pierced the night sky and warned citizens to quench all light that might emanate from their homes, our parents immediately rushed around the house, to check that all the lights were extinguished. They left one lamp burning in the living room— the only room outfitted with blackout shades through which no light could pass. They closed the sliding pocket doors between the living room and the dining room, as well as the door to the entrance hall.

The family gathered in the living room. Our parents calmly read beside the lamp as they waited for the drill to end. But I was apprehensive, imagining the Luftwaffe zooming across the water to pepper our town with incendiary bombs.

Each neighborhood had an air raid warden assigned to make sure that no light could be seen from any of the houses. Our warden was Mr. Lomenzo, who owned a shoe repair shop on Strawberry Street. He took his job seriously, as indeed he should have. Dressed in a steel helmet and carrying a flashlight and a billy club, he patrolled Fig Street in the dark until the all-clear signal sounded.

During one blackout, we were sitting in semi-silence in the living room. The radio was turned down low, as if we were concerned that the enemy might hear it and send a bomb our way. All of a sudden there was a loud, officious rapping at the front door. We froze. The Gestapo! No, it was only Mr. Lomenzo striking the door with his billy club to inform us that a tiny chink of light had escaped beneath one of our blackout shades.

from the coffeepot that Mother always kept warming on the stove indicated that there had been no disruption to the family's daily routine. We set our books on the table by the entrance and headed down the hall to the kitchen. The kitchen radio was turned on, as it usually was during the day; but instead of going about her chores while it played in the background, Mother stood in front of it, as if she could see the Norfolk station announcer advising listeners to prepare for a massive storm. Our brother, Jerry, unconcernedly pushed his toy truck across the floor.

Mother had placed a hurricane lamp in the center of the kitchen table and a pile of candles on the kitchen counter. While she was preparing our lunch of tomato soup and peanut butter and jelly sandwiches, the leaves on the walnut tree outside the kitchen window started to quiver uneasily. Then the sky darkened, and the tree branches began to sway. Suddenly the wind swept in. For several hours, it roared around the house. We heard the crack of tree limbs breaking in the heavy gale.

The electricity failed. The radio fell silent. Heavy rain drummed on the metal roof. I sat, drawing and coloring, at the kitchen table. In spite of the violence that swirled outside, I took comfort in knowing that I was sheltered at home.

By suppertime, the wind had died down, but it continued to rain. When it started to get dark, Mother lit the kerosene lamp. It threw a circle of light on the table and cast strange shadows into the corners of the room. Our father had not come home for supper at the usual time, and Mother was keeping his dinner warm in the gas oven. After a while, when he did not show up, she tried to call his office, but the phone was dead. That night, we prepared for bed by candlelight. Father still had not appeared.

When she thought that we were asleep, Mother took a flashlight and ran to the house of our next-door neighbor, Nanny Bette Kellam. Nanny Bette's husband, although well into his forties, had volunteered for the Naval Reserve. He was called up from time to time, and was presently at sea as a radio operator on a battleship. Mother was hoping that they might get some weather news through

HURRICANE

On Thursday, September 14, 1944, I was in Miss I
Lattimer's third-grade class. Late in the morning
teacher was called out of the classroom. When she ret
she very calmly addressed the class.

"Children, there's a hurricane coming. It should be here
want you to gather up your books and go home for the res'
day. Go straight home. Do not stop anywhere along the '
for those of you who live in the country, your parents ha
called and they are coming to pick you up. Now, town stude!
forget—this is important—you must go straight home!"

With a loud scraping of chairs and a buzz of excited excl
we gathered up our books. How thrilling to have this int
in our usual routine! Before leaving the school building
for Jane among the first-grade children, who, with mu
chattering, were lining up for dismissal.

Jane and I quickly walked the few blocks home unde
had taken on an unusual greyish-yellow appearance. The
The trees were still. The town was quieter than usual—aln
except for the insistent drone that insects make during
of summer. To me, their unremitting cacophony, like tl
small drill whirring, intensified the urgency of the me!
important—you must go straight home!" We hurried '

When I opened the front door, the familiar arom

the shortwave radio that Mr. Kellam kept at home. No sooner had Nanny Bette poured each of them a cup of tea than they heard a frantic rapping at the front door. When Mrs. Kellam opened the door, there was little Jerry standing on the front porch in his pajamas. He had awakened to find Mother gone, had panicked, and ran next door. Mother, abandoning any idea of using the shortwave radio, took Jerry home, changed him into dry pajamas, and put him back to bed.

An oily smell from the kerosene lamp still hung around the kitchen in the morning, but the rain had stopped. We rushed out onto the kitchen porch to view the damage wrought by the hurricane. Several huge poplar trees had toppled over and were strewn across the front lawn of our neighbors, the elderly Misses Bette, Nette, and Lou Nottingham.

Later that morning, our exhausted father, wearing his water-soaked hat and jacket, appeared at the kitchen door. Even though he was fifty-eight years old, he had been working all night helping to restore the systems that served the railroad and ferry complex. It was imperative, during World War II, that the important transportation link between the Eastern Shore and the military installations of Hampton Roads be kept intact. Father changed his clothes, ate breakfast, and then was out of the door for what would become several more days and nights of emergency electrical repair work in the harbors of Cape Charles and Norfolk. He also had to be sure that the signal system that served the railroad on the Virginia end of the Delmarva Peninsula was intact.

That afternoon, Mother put Jerry in the stroller, and we all went out to view the damage to the town. We carefully stepped around the utility lines still lying on the ground. Citizens were busily gathering up the debris around their homes and businesses. Others had volunteered to help the authorities remove obstructions from the roads and streets. Several of the people we met were quick to inform us that part of the school roof had been blown away. They knew we children would be interested in that news!

As usual after a heavy storm, we headed for the beach to see what the rough surf had deposited along the shore—maybe a big turtle, some interesting driftwood, or an old crate. To our amazement, a large naval landing craft had washed up and was embedded in the sand. Smaller vessels were called in to try to dislodge it. Standing among the spectators who lined the boardwalk, we heard citizens exchanging accounts of their hurricane experiences. To the general amusement of the crowd, one of the shopkeepers pointed out the irony that a landing craft which was specifically designed to unload troops and vehicles onto embattled shores should find itself stranded in the sand on the beach at Cape Charles.

LST Stranded on the beach in Cape Charles

DOWNTOWN

The term "downtown" might have implied something grander, but that was how many people who lived in Cape Charles referred to our one main shopping street. Most of the stores in Cape Charles were located on Mason Avenue—or "Front Street," as it was commonly called. Front Street was an extension of the main road leading into town and up to the railroad station. On one side of Front Street, an attractively landscaped park enhanced the view of the train station situated next to the harbor and docks. Much of the parking for the business district ran along the harbor side of the street. On the other side of Front Street, various shops, a bank, two movie theaters, and three drugstores served the retail needs of the community. Doctors' and a dentist's offices were located up narrow wooden staircases on the second floors of some of the businesses along Front Street.

Merchants on Mason Avenue drew customers from all over Northampton County. In addition to local trade, passengers from the trains that traveled up and down the peninsula patronized the drugstores and restaurants, as did those who were traveling by car. Business was especially brisk during World War II, when the troop trains halted across the street from the retail section. Soldiers and sailors would walk across the tracks in search of meals that were more palatable than the rations that had been issued to them on the train. In their hurry, they often just threw money onto the counters and left without waiting for their change.

Fort John Custis added over a thousand new soldiers to the area—and since their commissary was in Norfolk, many found it more convenient to do their shopping in Cape Charles. Uniformed soldiers were seen on the streets of town every day, and their presence added to the local economy.

The sidewalk on Mason Avenue was so busy on Saturdays that pedestrians had to walk out in the street. That was when the farm families drove to town to make their weekly purchases. The farmers congregated in Collins Hardware Store as they waited for their wives to finish shopping. If I happened to be in the hardware store on a summer afternoon, I could not help but hear the anxious buzz of the farmers' conversations. They speculated on the price of corn or whether the tomatoes from South Carolina would be ready to be shipped at the same time as theirs, inundating the market and reducing prices. At times, it sounded as if a little chunk of the Chicago commodities market had broken away and landed on Mason Avenue. The farmers followed the harvest returns attentively—and with good reason. Success in the northern produce markets could determine how well a farm family might live during the coming year.

On Saturdays in summer, the migrant farm workers were paid and came to town to shop. I loved to watch people from varied backgrounds fill the street and cram into the stores as, with an air of focused determination, they made their purchases for the coming week. If my father had business downtown on Saturday, I would ask to go along. While I waited for him in the car, I was intrigued by the sight of workers from Puerto Rico, Mexico, Haiti, the Bahamas, and the Deep South, all of whom gave Mason Avenue an exotic ambiance. The most eye-catching were the Seminole Indian women who had come up from Florida. With their black hair hanging down their backs in one long braid, colorful beads around their necks, and ankle-length multicolored skirts, they stood out among the more plainly dressed migrant workers the way brilliantly colored tropical birds might stand out among the dark foliage in the depths of a rain forest.

Observing the activities of others was one of the main spectator sports in Cape Charles. For that purpose, the old Virginia Hotel at the corner of Randolph Avenue and Strawberry Street was the perfect venue. With its overhanging second-story balcony, it had the outward appearance of a set from a western movie. At any time of day, sitting on benches beneath the balcony, a group of five or six retired men observed and discussed the comings and goings of their fellow citizens. This was the forum at which these unofficial jurists deliberated over all the happenings in the town. Most people who had business downtown walked or drove along Strawberry Street to get to Mason Avenue, and so passed by the Virginia Hotel. Whenever pedestrians approached, the men greeted them with courtesy. As the walker continued on, the sentinels at the Virginia Hotel were sure to comment about him or her, favorably—or maybe not so favorably.

Years later, during my travels in southern France, Italy, and Spain, I noticed that every village and town had a similar collection of elderly men sitting at the busiest spot on their community's main road, street, or plaza as they whiled away the hours overlooking the passing scene. Then I would think of Cape Charles, and those avid arbiters of social behavior who stationed themselves each day in front of the Virginia Hotel.

WILD CHERRY WINE

A graceful wild cherry tree near the rose garden was my favorite climbing tree. I used to sit up in its branches, just letting my mind wander in a rather idle way. One summer it became the centerpiece of a controversy that disrupted two households for several weeks.

Our next-door neighbor, Milson Kellam, and my father were inspired to make wine using the wild cherries that were always so abundant on that tree and the smaller one beside the back porch. This was surprising—because the Kellams, Milson and Nannie Bette, were strict Baptists who otherwise abhorred strong liquor; and Father had been raised in a temperance household. The Kellams were close friends of my parents, and occasionally they and a few other neighbors would gather at our house for an evening of music, with Mother playing the piano and the others standing nearby singing "In the Garden," "The Lost Chord," and old hymns and songs that one seldom hears anymore.

One of those evenings, a discussion arose as to whether wine could be made from the wild cherries growing in our yard. Two of the men decided to find out. The following Saturday morning, Mr. Kellam and my father picked the trees clean of cherries. For weeks afterward, the cherries fermented in two giant earthenware crocks on our back porch.

It was wartime, and civilians were entitled to buy limited amounts of sugar, gasoline, and other items that our armed forces needed. Every family was issued a book of rationing stamps and sugar coupons, both allotted on a yearly basis. When one bought sugar, he or she handed the shopkeeper the required number of coupons along with the purchase. Once the stamps or coupons were gone, the purchaser had to wait to buy sugar until the government issued new coupons. Needless to say, families were very careful with their sugar rations.

The wine recipe, however, required sugar, and my father and Mr. Kellam blithely turned in a large portion of their families' sugar rations for the project. This created hardship for their wives, who were counting on a certain amount of sugar for the family's needs and the summer canning. Mother's resentment over the lack of sugar was so great that, months after the wine had been bottled, we children made ourselves scarce whenever the subject of our sugar shortage arose.

Father set the bottles—it looked as if there were about a dozen of them—at the very front of one of the pantry shelves, where they could be easily admired. When the wine had aged for what he deemed to be a sufficient period of time, and with great ceremony, Father decided to open the first bottle.

The family gathered in the kitchen to witness the event. But as soon as the bottle was opened, a blackish-purple liquid shot out with such force that some of it actually ended up on the kitchen ceiling, and most of the rest fizzed down the sides of the bottle and onto the floor. Upon tasting the wine, my parents pronounced it unpalatable, and immediately poured the remaining contents down the drain. I never saw another bottle opened from that particular vintage. I think the rest of the bottles of wine ended up in the garbage, and my father seemed to abandon any further thoughts of becoming a vintner.

When I was fifteen, Father bought a casino that had been abandoned at the end of a pier that stretched into the Chesapeake Bay just beyond Washington Avenue. For a few years it had served as the town's ferry terminal, but it had been converted to a casino when the railroad installed its own terminal next to the train station. It was of extra sturdy construction, built to withstand high winds and wet weather. The wood framing and floor joists were covered with protective creosote. Father was having the casino remodeled to serve as our new residence. He had it moved to a lot on Monroe Avenue, from which we could look out at the horizon of the Chesapeake Bay and see the ships of the Old Bay Line making their way between Norfolk and Baltimore. He installed oak floors that he purchased from the old Chesapeake Hotel on Pine Street, which had recently been demolished.

Soon after moving the casino to its new location, and following a long and painful battle with cancer, Father died. He never complained about the suffering he endured while ill, but I do know that he worried over the fact that construction of the house had to cease. The house was under roof, the studs were in place, the electricity had been installed, as had the plumbing—yet much remained to be done. Shortly after his death, colleagues from the Cape Charles headquarters of the Pennsylvania Railroad formed a committee and, as a generous gift to my father's memory, completed the remaining work.

Nine years after the wine-making fiasco, we were able to move into the new house. While packing for the move, my mother found a bottle of the wartime wine that had survived at the back of a pantry shelf. She tossed it into a box with the rest of the groceries, and it came with us to our new home. As soon as the house was presentable, Mother invited friends and former neighbors to a housewarming party. Early in the evening, maybe on a whim, or maybe to include something from my father in the celebration, Mother decided to take a chance and open that last bottle of wild cherry wine. She cautiously pried off the seal. I held my breath, expecting the wine to erupt from the bottle and cast purple stains all over the new kitchen the way the first one had. But nothing happened. Mother brought the wine to the living room and poured small amounts into the adults' glasses. They raised a toast to my father and the new house. After taking the first few sips, everyone raved about the wine. It was proclaimed delicious. Nine years of aging had done the trick! Too bad there was only one bottle left.

THE SWAMP

In the field behind our house where my father planted his vegetables, Jane and I and other children from the neighborhood played boisterous games of "cowboys and Indians" or "cops and robbers." We chased each other through the high summer corn, and took beads on our opponents with our cap pistols from behind the outbuildings at the edge of the field. Then we would run to take cover somewhere else.

Sometimes we wandered off to play in the sand traps on the golf course of the Cape Charles Country Club. The golf course was located between our field and a wooded area that contained a small swamp, an extension of the Chesapeake Bay inlet called Kings Creek. Whenever we felt the need for a new adventure, we would slip into the swamp. Once inside, we left the big vistas of fields and sky and entered a secret sanctum of shadow, dark water, and small, wary creatures. We made our way carefully through the swamp by balancing on fallen trees. Most of the logs were covered with damp moss, and occasionally one of us would slip off a log and return home covered in silt and slime.

I had a classmate, Deanne Etz, with whom I was friends. I liked Deanne, but I envied her as well. Besides being pretty, with wavy black hair and long-lashed blue eyes, she was blessed with four older brothers who taught her how to compete with other children. She came to school already proficient at many of the sports and games to which the rest of us had not yet been introduced. The brothers helped her with her homework, called out her spelling words, and taught her to catch, throw, and hit a baseball. I, as the first child of older parents, was much less sophisticated.

One day when we were about eight years old, Deanne came home with me after school. She lived in another part of town, where folks were not familiar with the swamp. I figured Deanne would be as impressed with me as I was with her superior sports and academic skills if I showed her my "secret" place. At first, she was reluctant to set foot in such a wild entanglement of decaying woods. After much coaxing and encouragement, I was able to convince her to enter the swamp. Since, unlike me, she was not an old swamp hand, she immediately fell from a slippery log into the brackish water. As we climbed out of the swamp, she worried about what her mother would say to see her so wet and dirty.

When we got back to the house, my mother gave her a bath and, much to my dismay, sent her home in my favorite dress of cherry-printed fabric with a cluster of red cherries embroidered on the collar. Deanne's mother took the incident in good spirits, but Deanne never came to visit me again. I guess she wasn't as impressed with the swamp as I had hoped.

At night, the swamp, which seemed so silent during the day, came to life. Lying in bed, I could hear from beyond the fields and golf links the loud monotonous croaking of the bullfrogs in their watery habitat, the buzz of cicadas, and the drone of myriad insects—a symphony of summer sounds. Then, with an image of the mysterious swamp before me, I would drift off to sleep.

THE SWIMMING HOLE

Because the Chesapeake Bay was shallow off the shore at Cape Charles, an area where the water was normally chest-high had been excavated to provide a swimming hole. In August of 1945, the city fathers arranged to have the existing swimming hole dredged to make it larger and deep enough for diving. A new platform and diving board were erected as well.

The next summer, I was nine years old, and allowed to go into the water by myself. On the first hot summer's day, a crowd of young people gathered to try out the much-anticipated diving board and expanded swimming venue. Laughing and shouting, we ran through the shallow surf toward the deeper water. Delighted by the prospect of splashing among an older crowd, I threw myself into the swimming hole.

That day, no one realized that the new improvement had created a strong undertow. I was the first swimmer to be sucked into it.

Helpless to extract myself as I was drawn below, I tried to fight against the downward force. During my struggle to surface, I could see the events of my short life, like the projected images of a film, unrolling within my brain.

Fortunately, before I drowned, I was pulled out of the vortex by Mary Catherine Ames, our family physician's teenage daughter. After I recovered my breath, she asked if I was alright. I said yes, and continued to play in that dangerous place for the rest of the afternoon.

We soon learned to avoid the section of the hole that would pull us under. Unfortunately, several adults who were unaware of the undertow lost their lives in the swimming hole over the next few years. I continued to frequent this popular spot, and I secretly took pride in the fact that I had seen something no one else had—the replay of my life passing before my eyes.

I never told my parents about the near drowning incident, and though I only thanked her briefly at the time, to this day I am grateful to Mary Catherine Ames for saving my life.

EASTER, 1946

"I guess you got you'sef a new outfit for Easter."

"No, Mandy, we have to watch our expenses this year. I might be the only person in church without a new spring wardrobe."

"Well, Miss Joyce, dat's OK. Them other folks'es goin' to church to show off dey clothes. You goin' to praise de Lawd."

Mandy, who could always make you feel better with her comforting way of stating things, was helping Mother prepare for Easter. The house, which had been given an extra-thorough cleaning, was fragrant with furniture polish. A clove-studded ham slowly baked in the oven, and a big bouquet of snapdragons stood in a large vase on the hall table.

Our family had kept Lent, with a strict schedule of fasting that consisted of entrées such as baked fresh fish, oyster stew, oyster casseroles topped with buttered bread crumbs, succulent fried oysters, Maryland crab cakes, and mouth-watering macaroni and cheese casseroles made with sharp onion-flavored cheese. A variety of vegetables accompanied the main dishes. The dietary restrictions seemed to trigger Mother's creativity, so that Lenten meals turned out to be the most delicious meals of all. Dessert, however, appeared on Sundays only, which was unfair to us children, who were not expected to fast. Throughout Lent, we accompanied our mother to St. Charles Catholic Church for church services that culminated in the evening vigils of Maundy Thursday, Good Friday, and Holy Saturday.

The school had presented an Easter program for our parents the day we dispersed for spring break. When we gathered to plan for the production, the teacher in charge asked if any of us knew an Easter poem. Since my mother loved poetry and often read it aloud to her children, I could come up with a poem to suit most any occasion. I raised my hand, and since I already knew a poem, I was selected to recite it at the assembly. "The lilies are white in the Easter light, / The lilies with hearts of gold; / And they silently tell with each milk-white bell, / the story an Angel told . . ." As I stood before the assembly, I heard a classmate loudly whisper from one of the front seats, "Miss Priss." Apparently, having a poem ready for every event did not guarantee popularity.

On Good Friday and Holy Saturday, the only local florist made his trip from Onancock and Only, over thirty-five miles north of Cape Charles, to deliver the orders of corsages for the ladies' spring coats, centerpieces for the dining room tables, and flowers for the churches. I was enchanted when he arrived bearing our usual Easter bouquet of snapdragons. Imagine that! Flowers from a store!

One evening during Holy Week, our neighbor, Gertrude Post, glorying in the fact that sugar rationing had been lifted, marshaled several women of the neighborhood to make large chocolate-covered eggs as centerpieces for their children's Easter baskets. Mother asked me, the oldest child in the family, to accompany her to "Gertie's" kitchen, in case I was needed to help carry the eggs home. I watched in fascination as the women added chopped maraschino cherries, nuts, and tiny shavings of chocolate to batches of butter, cream cheese, and confectioner's sugar. They formed the stiff mixture into egg shapes six inches long, and when the eggs were chilled and firm, the ladies dipped them into a big pot of melted chocolate. What a good time they had, talking and laughing like young girls as, pastry tubes in hand, they decorated the eggs with pastel-tinted icing. Late that night, Mother and I walked home in the dark, each of us carefully carrying two beautiful eggs with the names—Patricia, Jane, Jerry, and James—written in icing on top of his or her egg.

That first Easter after the war, it seemed as if everyone made an extra-special effort to celebrate. As church bells rang out all over town, citizens, dressed in their spring finery, emerged from their homes. The churches were fragrant with the scent of white Easter lilies. At our church, a stately Easter candle at the front of the altar proclaimed the Resurrection. Fresh new paper fans, decorated with pictures of lilies and the name and phone number of the local undertaker, lay in the pews.

Our family slid into a pew from which we could admire the hats and corsages of the ladies when they entered the church. Some of the men sported new suits. My brother Jerry was neatly dressed in his navy blue Eton suit. Jane and I wore lightweight wool spring suits with pleated skirts and little straw hats. James, still a toddler, stayed at home with Father, who had attended an early-morning service. A few young men, recently demobilized from the army, were scattered among the congregation, but here and there, we spotted soldiers still in uniform.

The church was crowded, as it always was on Easter Sunday. Up in the choir loft, the organ played softly as the congregation seated itself. Then the music expanded to triumphal volume when the altar boys, followed by Father Miller, processed down the aisle. St. Charles had a loyal choir composed of singers—some of whom had been loyal for too many years—and since neither the priest nor the choir director had the courage to suggest that they retire, a few cracked voices were only to be expected. A moment of musical beauty, however, occurred during Communion, when the pure notes of "*Panis Angelicus*," rendered by Dot Leahy Robbins, seemed to hang in the air above the heads of the worshipers. At the end of the service, the congregation came to the aid of the choir by drowning them out with a rousing rendition of "Christ the Lord is Risen Today."

Back at home, we sat down to our Easter dinner, not forgetting to say grace and to ask God to bless our returning troops. As usual, our Easter Sunday meal included ham, asparagus, scalloped potatoes laced with lots of onions, a relish tray, tomato aspic, and hot rolls.

After dinner, much to my horror, Mother picked up a knife and sliced into Jerry's big chocolate Easter egg. She distributed pieces to each of us for dessert. So! We were not to be the sole proprietors of our holiday treats! I guess it was just too much to expect that Mother would entrust her children with such oversized confections to be devoured at will. The Big Eggs had been confiscated and were stored in the refrigerator only to appear after meals and judiciously distributed to all family members. The removal of the big eggs left our Easter baskets looking rather sparse.

In spite of the now skimpy Easter baskets, it had been a lovely Easter. With our country at peace, better times were surely on the way. How could we know that in 1946, for the first time in its history, the backbone of our community, the Pennsylvania Railroad, had operated at a loss?

THE BIG CHRISTMAS PARADE

Every December, the Cape Charles business district was traditionally festooned with fresh evergreens entwined with strings of multicolored Christmas lights. These garlands were hung across Mason Avenue and the business section of Strawberry Street. During World War II, many of the bulbs burned out, and there were no replacements available, as frivolities such as Christmas lights were not being manufactured. For several years during the War and afterward, as well, the downtown streets were practically bare of any holiday decor.

In 1948, colored Christmas bulbs had become available once more, so it was announced on the front page of the local weekly newspaper, *The Northampton Times*, that a committee of representatives from all the civic and service groups in Cape Charles had been formed to oversee the decorating of the business area. It was also announced that, as an antidote to the years of wartime austerity, an expanded Christmas celebration was being planned. The committee, now calling itself the Celebration Committee, elected Father Henry Miller as its chairman. He was the pastor of St. Charles Catholic Church and a football coach at Cape Charles High School. Since he knew most of the young people in town, he was in a position to solicit their help for the celebration projects.

Among the events to be sponsored was a turkey run, for which two turkeys a day would be released on Mason Avenue on the

Tuesday, Wednesday and Thursday before Christmas. Whoever caught a turkey could keep it for Christmas dinner.

The women's auxiliaries of the Cape Charles Fire Department and the American Legion arranged to have special mailboxes erected in front of the Radium and the Palace Theatres for the children's letters to Santa. While the contents of the letters would not be revealed, *The Northampton Times* offered to publish the names of all the children who sent one.

James Mulligan, the music director of Trinity Methodist Church, had an outdoor program of Christmas music planned for December 23rd which would utilize the combined choirs of several churches. There was to be a contest for the best-decorated home, and a Christmas parade the likes of which had never been staged in Cape Charles.

This parade, the crowning event of the season, was scheduled to take place on the afternoon of December 20th. Floats were being constructed to portray Snow White and the Seven Dwarfs, Old King Cole and his fiddlers three, the Old Woman Who Lived in a Shoe, Little Bo Peep, Li'l Abner, Cinderella, and most importantly, a Nativity scene. The Goddess of Liberty and the Spirit of '76, Donald Duck, Superman, and other comic book characters would also be included in the parade. The award-winning Chincoteague High School band agreed to make the trip from its island home to march in the parade, since Cape Charles did not have a band at that time. Santa Claus had been persuaded to ride the Fire Department's brand-new ladder truck and distribute candy to small children at the end of the parade.

The front page of the paper also carried a notice from the Merchant's Association stating that its participation in these events was not designed to bring people into the business district for commercial reasons, but a sincere desire to thank the members of the public for their support and patience during the wartime shortages.

Who would take the roles of the characters in the parade? Most of them were to be chosen from students at the school. A meeting was scheduled to assign places. In the week before the meeting, I could hardly come to a decision as to which character I might prefer. My first choice was Mary in the Nativity scene. If not, maybe an angel. Snow White would be good. Cinderella would probably go to a high school girl, and I was only in the fifth grade. Little Bo Peep was doubtful, if there were to be live sheep. Come to think of it, there might be sheep on the Nativity float. Well, they should be the responsibility of the shepherds.

At the meeting, Father Miller read out the roster of parts. Deanne Etz, one of my most attractive classmates, received the coveted role of Mary. My sister Jane and several other pretty girls were asked to be angels. So I was not to be on the Nativity float. Okay; there were other parts. Then, just as I expected, an attractive high school girl was given the Cinderella spot. The Goddess of Liberty went to another high school girl, but I didn't want that part anyway. Now the Dogpatch float called for a tall, good-looking high school boy to take the part of Li'l Abner, and an equally tall blonde to portray Daisy Mae. "Patricia Joyce, would you and Jack McCabe be Mammy and Pappy Yokum?"

What! Mammy Yokum! My heart sank. "Patricia, do you think your mother could make the costume? If not, let me know and I will get someone to run it up. Now for Snow White ... "

Several of my classmates giggled, pointed at me, and, with their childish sense of humor, whispered, "Mammy Yokum, Mammy Yokum!" How could they resist?

Mammy Yokum! I felt insulted to portray such an unattractive character. Was I picked because I was the ugliest girl in school? In spite of my pain, good sportsmanship, such as was constantly preached at home and at school, required that I accept the role with good humor, but secretly I despised myself for being considered the best person to portray an ugly hillbilly like Mammy Yokum. Later that day, behind the closed door of my bedroom, I burst into tears of anger and disappointment, while downstairs, my mother, delighted with the project, began planning my costume.

On the afternoon of December 20th, the ferry traffic was diverted away from Mason Avenue onto one of the side streets. Our fully decorated main street was lined with most of the town's residents. Jack McCabe, as Pappy Yokum, and I took our places behind a float covered with bales of hay, upon which the two tall high school students representing Li'l Abner and Daisy Mae lounged in lazy Dogpatch fashion beside a sign that read "Dogpatch," which was the home of those popular comic strip characters.

A burning feeling of humiliation invaded my entire body as I appeared wearing a brown paper grocery bag, which my mother had painted black and fashioned to resemble Mammy Yokum's outlandish hat. I clenched a corncob pipe in my teeth as I struggled to walk in the pair of Mother's old galoshes that had been stuffed with newspaper so they would stay on my feet. Indeed they did resemble Mammy Yokum's outsized shoes, especially when pulled on over the ridiculous striped stockings that, along with a miniscule black skirt, completed the Mammy Yokum look. How I wished I could just become invisible!

After the parade, clusters of citizens lingered to chat and critique the parade, to admire the Chincoteague High School band with a touch of envy, and to wish each other a happy Christmas. Several people came up to my mother and complimented her on the authenticity of my costume. I really looked like Mammy Yokum. I smiled my good-sportsmanship smile while giving angry little nods of thanks for the compliments. Mrs. McCabe said that I had presented my part to perfection—but little did she know that I carried off a far more difficult role than that of Mammy Yokum. I realized then that good sportsmanship, like virtue, has to be its own reward.

ALONG THE CREPE MYRTLE TRAIL

On many weekend afternoons in the late 1940s, Mother, Jane and I walked to the village of Cheriton, four miles north of Cape Charles. We ambled along at a leisurely pace, noting details, such as which crops were maturing in the fields, which wildflowers were in bloom, and the variety of grasses that sprang up along the road. We commented on things that often went unnoticed when we sped along Route 13 by auto: the rich color of goldenrod in autumn, the delicate design of Queen Anne's lace, the insistent heartiness of ordinary weeds. We discussed each plant's unique, if underrated, beauty.

During July and August, our route was graced by a line of pink crepe myrtle trees heavy with blooms. Several times on our walk, Mother expressed her appreciation for the generosity of those who had planted these trees for the enjoyment of the public. Then her expressions of admiration for the crepe myrtle plantings would segue into a lecture, aimed at Jane and me, about the importance of making a contribution to one's community.

In the fall of 1925, under the leadership of Miss Kate Savage and Mrs. Curry Thomas, and with the support of the State Highway Commission, the Northampton County Woman's Club began a project to plant crepe myrtle trees on either side of the highway. They placed their first order for the trees. Then, one Saturday noon in autumn, the young trees were delivered to Miss Savage in Cape

Charles. Anxious to get them planted right away rather than hold them until Monday (working on Sunday being unthinkable), she called on a group of the ladies to help. Miss Savage also appropriated the aid of field hands from her brother's farm. Together, they got the first trees safely into the ground.

The Accomack Chapter of the Eastern Shore Woman's Club was established in 1925. As one of its first projects, it joined the Northampton Woman's Club in planting crepe myrtle trees along Accomack County's portion of Route 13. Soon, an unbroken row of cotton-candy-pink crepe myrtles was in place from Bayview, south of Cape Charles, to the Maryland state line, seventy miles north. For many years, the trees thrived, adding beauty to an otherwise uninteresting commercial route and providing a pleasing sight from the windows of the passing trains.

In 1929, Miss Kate Savage wrote a poem about planting the trees:

THE PRIVATE IN THE RANKS

An idea sprang into being, in the fall of '25,
That the club should plant some trees along the public drive.
After many hot discussions and arguments pro and con
For all the trees one could think of, the gay Crape Myrtle won.
So from out its proud seclusion, an aristocrat of a by-gone day,
It took its place in modern life
In the form of battle array.
Flaunting its crinkly banners, not behind some garden wall,
But with the spirit of true democracy, in sight of one and all.
But what of the workers who toiled in sunshine, wind or rain,
Who grubbed and dug and planted, and dug and planted again?
Alas 'tis the way of the world; a brief moment and they are no more;
But the trees will be living monuments, to the Woman's Club of the Eastern Shore.

When I was a child, the trees flourished. But when a malaise fell over the Shore's economy in the 1960s, they were neglected. Over the years, choked by honeysuckle and weeds, some died; but many have remained to this day. The powerful Pennsylvania Railroad is gone, and the once-busy ferries have long ceased to ply the Chesapeake Bay, but what remains of the crepe myrtle trail continues its brave struggle for survival along the highway.

But I digress. Once we got to Cheriton, we hurried into Paul's Restaurant for a cool drink and the use of Paul's pay phone to call Daddy to come and drive us back to Cape Charles.

A Good Read Was Always Welcome

Every evening after dinner, my parents sat reading their favorite books in the living room, while we children preferred to listen to radio programs such as "Inner Sanctum," which presented a weekly horror story, or "Camel Caravan," a musical hour sponsored by Camel cigarettes. On Saturday night, we couldn't wait to hear the "Old Dominion Barn Dance" broadcast from Richmond, Virginia; and "Grand Ole Opry" from Nashville, Tennessee. Sometimes, our mother would interrupt us and force us to listen to poetry by the New England poets or Edgar Allan Poe.

Before we learned to read, the bedtime story was our first introduction to literature. It included a heavy dose of poetry, especially works by Eugene Field from his *Poems of Childhood*, a large edition with beautiful illustrations by Maxfield Parrish. My favorite Eugene Field poem was "Wynken, Blynken, and Nod." Another of his poems that our parents read to us, "The Gingham Dog and the Calico Cat," dealt with the death of a child—rather unsettling verses to read to one's children at bedtime. My favorite book of poetry was *Chimney Smoke* by Christopher Morley. "The Balloon Peddler," which warns a peddler that some killjoy might sneak up behind him and prick his balloons with a pin, and "Animal Crackers," in which "Daddy once said, he would like to be me / Having cocoa and animals once more for tea!" were among my favorites. Some of Morley's poems were as melancholy as Field's, but then, isn't most poetry sad?

We preferred to have Mother read to us. Father read in a rather jerky manner. I did not realize that he was dyslexic (a condition that was not recognized at the time) until I had a child of my own who read in the very same way. Father did appreciate literature in spite of his dyslexia, but he mostly enjoyed his subscriptions to *The Southern Planter* and *Flower Grower* magazines.

The Saturday Evening Post and *Collier's*, popular monthly periodicals, were also delivered to our house. Once I became a proficient reader, I read the short stories and serials that ran in both publications. I especially looked forward to each episode of C. S. Forester's "Horatio Hornblower," a series that ran for many years in *The Saturday Evening Post.* Living in an area surrounded by water and boats, I felt that I could relate to those seafaring sagas.

Another publication we children loved was that enormous dream-book, the Sears, Roebuck & Company catalog, which arrived twice a year in the mail. We paged through the catalog, and imagined ordering items we wanted, knowing full well that they would never be ours. We ordered a new car for our parents, the latest bicycles for ourselves, clothes, a tractor for our father, a radio for each of us. There was no end to our desires, as suggested by Sears and Roebuck. We learned that some of the houses in Cape Charles had been delivered on the train, having been ordered from the Sears, Roebuck & Company catalog. We laughed at the photos of models displaying underwear. When the new catalog arrived, we cut out pictures of the clothing models from the old catalog and played with them as if they were paper dolls. Once a package came that was addressed to me. It contained my first pair of jeans and a fielder's glove—straight from Sears and Roebuck!

Cape Charles' municipal library, at the corner of Tazewell Avenue and Plum Street, was housed in a former Presbyterian church that had become too small for its congregation. Half-day kindergarten was held there for any five-year-olds whose parents chose to enroll them. Attending kindergarten was not a requirement for first-grade registration, so there was no attempt to teach us to read and write. We simply enjoyed coloring, crafts, and the stories the kindergarten teacher read to us. I loved to sit quietly at a long table and work in the soft light that filtered through the Gothic arched windows. And how thrilled I was when I was invited to apply for my very own library card!

Mother must have read most of the books in the municipal library by the time I entered the sixth grade, because she began to request that I bring home books she wanted to read from the school library. Since Cape Charles High School included all grade levels, its library was well stocked with books appropriate for readers of every age. Mother especially admired the writings of F. Scott Fitzgerald and the English travel writer, H. V. Morton. By supplying her with reading material, I developed an undeserved reputation as a precocious reader.

One year—I must have been in the fifth or sixth grade—our teacher, Mrs. Chandler, told the class that if we behaved and finished our work in time, she would spend the last hour of the day reading us stories and poems by Edgar Allan Poe. We loved Poe's writing, especially the scary parts. What puzzled me was that Mrs. Chandler took the trouble to read from a French language collection of Poe's works, fluently translating his writing into English as she went along. Many years later, I attended a lecture sponsored by the Poe Museum in Richmond. The speaker, a Poe scholar, mentioned that the French never understood why Edgar Allan Poe was not as celebrated in the United States as he was in France, where he was considered one of the world's great authors. I learned that the works of Poe had been translated from English into French by Stéphane Mallarmé and by Charles Baudelaire, both among the finest of French writers. These translations far exceeded Poe's original writings in excellence. Mrs. Chandler must have known that fact and chosen to present the best to her students.

That year we read the *Odyssey* and the *Iliad*—in English, of course. How vivid the journeys of the ancient Greek mariners seemed to me! In my mind's eye, I visualized them on the Chesapeake Bay, making their way from Baltimore to Norfolk; caught on the Bay by a nor'easter; made captive on Smith Island; or lured by Sirens to a place like Tangier Island. I am amazed at how much our class looked forward to those ancient narratives.

Several years after I graduated from Cape Charles High School, I traveled with a friend as we toured Italy. We took a ferry to Sicily. As we crossed the Straits of Messina, I felt a thrill of excitement when some of my fellow passengers, natives of the region, pointed out those characters from the *Odyssey*: the treacherous rocky outcrop, Scylla; and the whirlpool, Charybdis. Good stories live on.

THE GREEN BEAN CAPER

The growing season on the Eastern Shore lasted a long time. Strawberries, the earliest crop, were harvested in May, and broccoli, cut in December, was the last crop of the year. Potatoes, tomatoes, corn, and green beans were some of the major farm products. Summer was a hectic time for farmers as they hastened to get their produce to market while keeping a careful watch on the maturation of crops in other regions of the South. When prices were good, money flowed into the farmers' bank accounts. But if the agricultural markets became flooded with a certain type of produce, prices for that fruit or vegetable plummeted, and a season's hard work would generate disappointing returns.

The farmers were often generous to the people who lived in town, especially when prices were low. Then townspeople could buy bushels of vegetables directly from the farms at little cost. Many a pantry shelf in town was laden with home-canned goods that reflected the success of that year's harvest.

One of my best friends at school was Merita Long. She lived on a large farm in lower Northampton County. Merita's parents occasionally invited me to spend several days at the farm as company for their daughter, and because Merita's parents made my visits exciting, I was always eager to go.

I was enthralled by the creativity of her attractive mother. One evening shortly before Christmas when Merita and I were in the third grade, Mrs. Long invited our entire class to a dinner party at her house. The dining room table had been expanded to accommodate all fifteen of us. It was beautifully set in a formal style, and to everyone's delight, shimmering Christmas trees made of green Jell-O sat on small plates beside each child's place. Mrs. Long had poured Jell-O into cone-shaped paper cups. After the Jell-O congealed, she placed the cones, top side down, on the small plates. When she peeled the cups away, behold, there were trees with fruit cocktail showing through the Jell-O like Christmas tree ornaments.

A few years later, I stayed with the Long family over New Year's weekend. Merita's fun-loving father promised that we would be treated to a beautiful midnight display of fireworks on New Year's Eve. All day long, our anticipation grew as Merita and I and her younger brother, Edwin, talked about the pending event. After dinner, we played charades, then cards, then Monopoly while we waited for the new year to arrive. As the evening wore on, we found ourselves nodding off over the Monopoly board. Mrs. Long decided that she would not stay up to celebrate New Year's Eve and suggested that we take a short nap, then get up in time to go outside and enjoy the fireworks.

When he was ready to set off the display, Merita's father called from the foot of the stairs to announce that it was almost midnight, but we were too leaden with sleep to budge. From beneath the comfort of our blankets, we heard the bang, boom, and hiss of fireworks breaking the silence of the winter night. Undaunted by the lack of an audience, Mr. Long, surrounded by miles of empty fields and woods, welcomed the new year with an extravagance of sound, color, and light.

Ever a farmer at heart, my father used to rent several acres of vacant land behind our house to cultivate whatever vegetable or flower took his fancy. One summer when I was twelve years old, he planted a field of green beans. When his green beans were ready for harvesting, he drafted my sister and me to help with the picking, because he wanted to get his beans to the northern markets before they were flooded with beans from South Carolina. Jane and I were not happy to be picking beans in the hot sun as we tried to avoid touching the little greenish-yellow caterpillars that hid among the leaves and that we considered repulsive.

Father took the bushels of beans that we had picked to the train station, where he discovered that the market was so overloaded with green beans that he could get little or nothing for them. He may have been working with a produce dealer—I don't know—but he was able to load the beans onto the train and send them north. He did not try to ship any more of the maturing beans to market that summer. Instead he picked what was left and, for as long as his vines were producing, tried to distribute the beans to his neighbors, friends, coworkers, or anyone who would accept them.

Shortly after our bean-picking ordeal, Merita invited me to stay with her family for several days. I was delighted with the invitation and happy to be excused from my own family's discouraging agrarian pursuits. Merita and I whiled away the days by playing cards, listening to records, and driving around in an ancient Cadillac that her parents allowed her to use with the understanding that we restrict our driving to the farm. How grown-up I felt as we wove along the dirt roads with the car windows down and the radio blasting out the latest hit tunes.

On the last day of my visit, Merita's father took us with him while he went on his errands. We sat in the back of his pickup truck, wind whipping our hair about our faces, as he went from his packing house to a produce-loading depot beside a rail spur and on to a dusty field where farm workers were busily digging potatoes. He then drove down to Fort Custis, at the very southern tip of the cape. The sentry at the gate casually waved us into the base, which was almost deserted now that the war was over.

Mr. Long gave us a tour of a large stretch of vacant land that had been farmland until the government confiscated it when they built Fort John Custis. The vacant land now served as a security buffer for the fort. Mr. Long pulled up in front of a deserted farmhouse that, he explained, used to be the home of family members of Virginia's Governor Wise, an Eastern Shore hero who had served as a Confederate general in the War Between the States. Though located within the perimeters of the fort, the house was away from the military installations. In spite of the structure's broken windows; its porch roof, which had caved in; and its front door, which hung open, it was obvious that it had once been a beautiful home. Small flakes of paint still clung to the exterior. There it sat in the high weeds, like one of the derelict boats we so often saw abandoned at the edge of a marsh.

When it was time to take me back to Cape Charles, the ever-kindly Mr. Long presented me with two large grocery bags to give to my parents. They were filled with—you guessed it—green beans! How could he have imagined that a town family had also planted several acres of the green beans that, like his, had matured at the wrong time? I was thoroughly sick of green beans, but I thanked him politely and carried some of his overabundance of green beans home to add to our own overabundance. At the same time, I wondered if bags and bushels of green beans were being passed in a circuit from family to family throughout the community.

Night Sky

On summer nights, our family liked to sit on the boardwalk and watch as the big orange sun reluctantly slipped beneath the horizon, sending back a final, defiant burst of light. Then that most serene heavenly body, the evening star, appeared in the afterglow of the western sky as a solitary herald of night. Twilight slowly faded to a streak of ocher at the edge of the earth. Then the sky became a black velvet canopy, seemingly so close that one might reach up and touch the icy stars. "Where's the North Star?" "There's the Big Dipper!" "Look! There's the Little Dipper!" "Isn't the Milky Way thick tonight?" An occasional shooting star might slide across the firmament and, once in a while, the heavens came alive with a meteor shower. What delight! What terror! What theater! There we sat, face to face with infinity, awestruck by the majesty of the night sky.

We were often the only people on the beach on summer nights, but on the Fourth of July, a generous fireworks display brought people from all across the county to the beachfront at Cape Charles. At dusk, with the annual fireman's carnival in full swing on a vacant plot nearby, spectators began to choose places from which to watch the fireworks. They spread blankets on the beach or settled themselves on the sand. Those who arrived early occupied the pavilion and benches on the boardwalk.

Around ten o'clock, the fireworks began. With my family, I sat on the beach, enchanted by the spectacle as plumy bursts of color and light hung in the air for a few seconds and then faded, while the next boom launched a new chrysanthemum into the sky.

Of course, I enjoyed every minute of the fireworks event—not the noise, but the excitement of seeing the crowd, the pyrotechnicians making last-minute adjustments, and the festive holiday atmosphere. But no fireworks could compare with watching the sky on a starry night and thinking how wonderful it is that we are part of this magnificent galaxy. Awesome!

Railroad Days

Because our father worked for the Pennsylvania Railroad, my parents had railroad passes that entitled them to travel, without paying, on the lines that the railroad served. Over the years, our family, taking advantage of that benefit, made a few trips by rail.

Several summers when I was in elementary school, the family visited Father's sister, Aunt Margaret, at her farm in Pennsylvania. How excited we always were, as we watched the hissing train's engine being prepared to leave the station in Cape Charles. And how annoyed we were when children who lived along the lane that led to Aunt Margaret's home called out to one another when they saw us dragging our suitcases up her hill: "The you-alls are here! The you-alls are here!" They couldn't even pronounce "y'all" properly—a sure indication that we were now on foreign soil.

In 1944, Mother took me with her to Philadelphia to buy rugs. Shortly before Thanksgiving, we boarded the train for the six-hour ride. This train was different from the more luxurious one Mother had taken to Cape Charles in 1936. To meet the exigencies of wartime, most trains had been stripped of unneeded amenities such as dining cars with white tablecloths, flowers, and Pennsylvania Railroad place settings of monogrammed china and silver. There were none of the old fashioned Pullman stewards who knew how to handle matters with elegance. Instead, the railroad's one objective was to move its increased load of military and civilian passengers efficiently to their destinations. The day we left for Philadelphia, I saw troop trains, filled to capacity, flash by our window as they headed for the Cape Charles ferries that would transport their passengers across the Chesapeake Bay.

Once in Philadelphia, Mother and I took a taxi to the home of a lady with whom Mother had gone to school. We spent the night with Mother's friend, and in the morning, the shopping marathon began. Before setting out, Mother told me that if I behaved and was patient while she shopped, she would treat me to a trip to the zoo at Fairmont Park.

Our search for the rugs began at John Wanamaker's Department Store. As we approached the main entrance to John Wanamaker's, a beautiful window display caught our attention. Within the display, a life-sized mechanical Santa Claus sat in a rocking chair next to a fireplace. As he rocked, he slapped his knees and emitted a big bass "Ho, ho, ho." Mother expressed amazement: "My goodness, Christmas decorations up already! We haven't gotten through Thanksgiving yet." (Mothers often speak of "getting through" a holiday.)

Mesmerized by the mechanics of the scene, we stood in admiration before the window for a good ten minutes. Then we passed through the front door and into a fairyland of elaborate red velvet and gold Christmas decor. From floor to ceiling, the great pipes of an organ dominated the wall at one end of the first-floor concourse. Mother told me that the pipes were part of a famous organ, the largest in the world, and that if we came back at noon, we could attend a concert.

Not to be deterred from her mission by the holiday artistry all around us, we went straight to the rug department. To me, the rug-buying process seemed to last for several hours. I shifted from one aching leg to another, weary from standing, while the patient salesman turned back rug after rug for Mother's inspection. After she finally made a selection, Mother gave the salesman instructions for shipping the rug to Cape Charles on the train. Then we were free to have lunch. But first, we returned to the concourse to hear the great organ.

The familiar music of the Christmas season filled the huge hall with a rich melody. After each piece ended, shoppers and others who had dropped in to listen broke into applause. When the concert was over, Mother and I rode the elevator to the tearoom to rest our legs and relax over a good lunch. Later that afternoon, Mother hailed a taxi to take us to the zoo—but, having slept poorly in the noisy city, and fatigued from a day of shopping, I was too tired to summon up much enthusiasm for a long walk through Fairmont Park.

In 1952, Mother, Jane, and I took the train to New York to see the Christmas program at Radio City Music Hall. We spent the first day trying to cram in as much sightseeing as possible, including a boat trip to Staten Island and an awe-inspiring ascent to the top of the Empire State Building, the tallest building in the world at that time. We stopped for lunch at the self-service Horn and Hardart Automat. As we entered, we were confronted by a wall of little glass doors, behind which a large selection of sandwiches, pies, cakes, and other cold items were displayed. After making my decision, I put nickels into the slot beside the chosen item, turned a knob that opened the glass door, and retrieved my sandwich.

The next afternoon, we attended a movie at Radio City Music Hall. When the movie ended, a line of long-legged dancers in red-and-white costumes high-kicked their way onto the stage. This was the famous precision dance troupe, the Rockettes, who, to my delight, presented the most eye-filling performance I had ever seen. Thanks to the railroad, I was able to ascend the tallest building in the world, see the Statue of Liberty resolutely standing in the New York harbor, and marvel at the famous Rockettes.

The Pennsylvania Railroad found itself operating in the red in 1946, and it gradually started to curtail its operations until the last passenger train left Cape Charles' station in 1957. Three years later, the railroad, responding to a request from the Cape Charles Town Council, employed a salvage company to demolish and remove its abandoned properties. The waiting room, where so many passengers used to anticipate stepping up into a coach that would carry them to their destinations, was gone. The terminal, from which a fleet of ferries connected our modest Mason Avenue with the large commercial enterprises on Granby Street in Norfolk, was gone. Of the railroad's office building, roundhouse, and shops, not a trace remained—only the memories.

The Richardson house at Kings Creek Marina

KINGS CREEK

Cape Charles' marina is located at the northern end of the residential district, at the mouth of Kings Creek, a large inlet off the Chesapeake Bay. It has always been a busy place, especially in summer, when pleasure boats pull into the marina for berthing, repairs, and provisions. During my teen years, the Kings Creek Marina was managed by Captain Ernest Richardson and his wife, Clara. Captain Richardson, a tall, handsome grandfather, owned several fishing boats. If you wanted to host a fishing party, he or his employee, Captain Parks, could be engaged to take you out of Kings Creek, down the Chesapeake Bay, past the Virginia Capes, and into the ocean for a day of deep-sea fishing.

When I was in the seventh, eighth and ninth grades, several bullies, mostly from the class ahead of mine, chose me as their victim. Two of the girls routinely threatened to beat me up. I was thankful that they never tried to do so, as I was small for my age and would have fared badly against them. Whenever they saw me, they taunted me, making fun of the way I walked. I did not know how to respond to such rudeness, so I tried to avoid them—but that's not an easy thing to do in a small town. While I was a target of the bullies, my former friends found it prudent to distance themselves from me. During those years, I sought solace in reading and in solitary activities, such as boating along Kings Creek.

One summer day, I was feeling especially lonely and ostracized. I felt I had to have a change of scene, so I walked the quarter mile down Fig Street, unmoored the old rowboat I kept along the shore by Kings Creek Marina, and pushed off into the water.

The creek was peaceful and scenic. Branches of some of the trees that lined the creek hung low over the water. An occasional small perch flipped up, and with faint plopping sounds, reentered the water, leaving little disturbance on the surface. There was comfort in the beauty that surrounded me. *Yes,* I reflected, *the loveliest scenes on the Eastern Shore are found along its inlets.*

Later, I pulled my boat ashore at the head of Kings Creek. I climbed up the bank, drawn by the remains of a graveyard that overlooked the water. It was a family burial site that had been part of an old plantation called Tower Hill. Among the weathered markers stood a monument to a woman named Maria Read, who had apparently died in childbirth. Next to her grave, a small tombstone bore the name of her child, who had died having lived but one day. Maria died a few days later.

I sat there to rest, and although I did not know Maria's history, I found myself thinking about her short life and wishing that she had lived to raise her child. After a while, I left Maria and rowed back down the creek, pondering the unfathomable questions of life that contemplation of Maria's grave had posed: death, suffering, and injustice. What did it all mean?

I decided to visit the Richardsons at the house from which they managed the marina. At the end of the pier, built over the creek, was an ample frame house with a living room, bathroom, bedrooms, and kitchen. Although they owned property in the town of Cape Charles, this was where they chose to live year-round. I decided to visit them. I knew that if Mrs. Richardson was at home, her cheerful conversation would help dispel the melancholy thoughts with which

I had just burdened myself. I also expected that she would offer me something to drink, as I was thirsty from rowing.

The Richardsons had a granddaughter, Marcia Sue Ferguson, a beautiful strawberry blonde. Attracted by all the activity of the marina and the welcome they found from their grandparents, she and her brother George Ronald spent much of their time with the Richardsons on Kings Creek. Marcia Sue was my sister Jane's classmate, and one of her best friends. Jane had spent the previous night with Marcia Sue at her grandparents' home on the creek, and she was still with them when I tied my boat to the pier.

As expected, Mrs. Richardson offered us glasses of lemonade. She also gave us slices of homemade cake. Jane told me she was too tired to eat her cake, and that she wanted to go home. "Be polite, and finish your cake," I whispered. She did, and then, after thanking the Richardsons for their hospitality, we left.

As we walked home together, Jane, unaccustomed to being out on the creek overnight, confided that she was exhausted because she hadn't slept well. "I could hear water moving under the house all night long." We walked further down the road. A few minutes later, she added, "I kept thinking about all those fish that were swimming under my bed."

I stopped and looked at Jane. We burst out laughing, and continued to chuckle all the way home. My spirits had been restored. What better treatment for "the blues" than physical exertion in a beautiful place, followed by a refreshing drink, a delicious piece of cake, and a good laugh?

By the time I was sixteen, much to my surprise, most of my awkwardness had disappeared. The students who had bullied me must have matured as well, because I was no longer an object of their ridicule—and it may have helped that I had acquired a big strong boyfriend. I spent less time sitting around reading, and with an improved social life, I no longer took my boat out into Kings Creek. But I will always be grateful for the comfort I found there during one of my life's difficult periods.

Deliver Us from Eastville

Two communities in Northampton County are listed on the National Register of Historic Places: the town of Cape Charles, and the village of Eastville. Most of the houses in Cape Charles were built in the late 1800s and early 1900s. The town has a turn-of-the-century appearance. It was the kind of place where one could picture the porches and shops draped with red, white and blue bunting on the Fourth of July. Cape Charles was once the major transportation and commercial center for Northampton County, as evidenced by the business district on Mason Avenue that runs the length of the town, and its deep harbor, which once served a busy ferry terminal. That a railroad was the original reason for the town's existence is no longer obvious.

Eastville, nine miles north of Cape Charles, has a different ambiance that is decidedly eighteenth century. It is the county seat of Northampton County, and contains its courthouse, law offices, county jail, sheriff's office, and records repository. The community centers on a courthouse green, where the county records have been recorded without a break since 1632. The court started meeting in an Eastville tavern during the 1600s, and it has remained the place from which justice has been meted out and county taxes collected ever since. Brick buildings of Classical design from the Georgian and Federal periods give the village an aristocratic aura. Many of the homes in Eastville and the surrounding countryside date from the mid-1700s to the early 1800s.

One of my mother's closest friends, Margaret Custis, lived on a farm in Savage Neck, which meant that she resided in the Eastville district. The ancestors of her husband, Rufus Custis, had farmed the land for many years. Their property on Savage Neck included Point Farm, which was situated at the end of Savage Neck Road on a beautiful site between Cherrystone Inlet and the Chesapeake Bay. Although the Custises lived in a more modern home on another part of their property, Point Farm boasted a second house dating from 1750.

After a run of disappointing harvests in the 1930s, the Custises sold Point Farm. When it came up for sale again in the mid-1940s, Mr. Custis desperately wanted to buy it back. Instead, it was purchased by an affable insurance agent, George Ames, who moved into the eighteenth-century house. Shortly after the second sale of Point Farm, while Mr. Custis was cleaning his hunting rifle, it accidently fired, killing him immediately. Later, Mrs. Custis told Mother that, after her husband died, she was glad they had sold Point Farm. Mr. Ames looked in on her from time to time, and it was a comfort to have an attentive neighbor on that lonely neck of land.

Mrs. Custis had a collection of fine antiques. (Only furniture manufactured before the end of the Federalist Period was considered antique in those days.) Her neighbors on the other side of Savage Neck Road lived at Kirwanton, a period home built around 1800. Whenever Kirwanton, as a typical Eastern Shore "big house, little house, colonnade and kitchen"-style home, was featured on Virginia's Historic Garden Week tour, Mrs. Custis loaned its owners some of her antiques. While the house was open to the public, it was even more authentically furnished than usual.

Mother and Mrs. Custis liked to make occasional visits to antiques stores up and down the Eastern Shore. Late one afternoon, as I sat in the living room, comfortably reading in Father's big easy chair, I heard the front door slam. Mother was home from one of their antiquing forays. She burst into the room so flustered she had to lie down on the couch. Alarmed by her agitated state, I ran to the kitchen and brought her a glass of cold water.

After she felt calm enough to speak, Mother recounted how she and Mrs. Custis had been driving from one antiques store to another when their car stalled on a railroad track that had no crossing gate. Suddenly a train appeared, whistle blowing as it sped toward them. Sure that this was to be her final hour, Mother started to pray out loud, while her friend frantically tried to get the car to start. The train was almost upon them when the ignition finally fired, and Mrs. Custis jumped the car off the tracks just as the train whizzed by. On the way home, in an attempt to lighten the mood, she remarked to Mother, "You do realize, don't you, that last minute prayers don't count?" That poor engineer! I sure hope someone thought to bring *him* a drink of cold water—or even something stronger.

Five years after we were married, my husband and I moved from Alexandria to Richmond. Before we left, Mrs. Custis gave me the name and phone number of her son Edward and his wife Mildred, who also lived in Richmond. She suggested that we contact them. After we got settled, I telephoned, and they invited me to their house for drinks. When the conversation turned to Eastville, Mildred Custis, who had grown up in Richmond, let me know exactly what she thought about the Eastern Shore—she hated it. She told me that she found life there to be boring, but mostly she objected to the large insect population. "I've never seen as many bugs as they have over there." She went on to confide that she got "eaten up by mosquitoes" whenever she set foot in Eastville. She then laughed and told me a funny story.

When her son Edward III was small, each night before he got into bed, he knelt to say the Lord's Prayer. At times, she felt that there was something disconcerting about his prayer. One night she listened carefully and heard:

> "Our Father who art in heaven,
> hallowed be thy name.
> Thy kingdom come.
> Thy will be done
> on earth as it is in heaven.

Give us this day our daily bread,
and forgive us our trespasses,
as we forgive those who trespass against us,
and lead us not into temptation,
but deliver us from Eastville."

Mildred agreed, "I say amen to that!"

Refreshment stand at the corner of Randolph and Bay Avenues.

Hot Dogs

The beach was a social center for teenage students at Cape Charles High School. There, in the silt-scented air of spring or the heat of a summer afternoon, the town's adolescents and the young men from Cape Charles Air Force Station spread their blankets, turned on their portable radios, and basted themselves with coconut oil or a mixture of baby oil and iodine.

In the early 1950s, the Etz family operated the Kool Korner, a refreshment stand across the street from the beach. They sold soft drinks, candy, and ice cream, but the most-appreciated items offered at the Kool Korner were the hot dogs. One couple I met there on a Sunday afternoon said that the Kool Korner had the best hot dogs on "The Shore." As they heaped chopped onions on their hot dogs, the couple told me that they lived further up the county, and that every weekend, they drove for miles to Cape Charles to treat themselves to Etz's hot dogs.

I learned the simple secret to better hot dogs the day I agreed to stand behind the counter for Deanne Etz for a couple of hours. I learned that the Etz family cooked the hot dogs for a short time in water, put each in a bun, wrapped them in paper, and placed them in a little electric oven. The warmth of the oven gave the buns a slight crispness on the outside, and the hot dog and bun stayed hot.

Now, when I prepare hot dogs, I copy the Kool Korner. I put the cooked hot dogs into the rolls, which I toast slightly, and place them in a warm oven for a while. If I'm feeling really generous, I heat the catsup, mustard, and relish, and serve it all hot. Each time I do this, I think of the Kool Korner, the long afternoons on the beach at Cape Charles, and the blended aromas of salt air, coconut oil, and chopped onions.

Boys jumping off the coal chute

Along the Railroad Tracks

Those of us who grew up during the railroad days generally agree that Cape Charles was a wonderful place in which to be young. As children, we freely roamed the community. We were welcomed everywhere as long as we behaved with decorum and did not interfere with the town's economic activities. If one of us stepped out of line, we received an immediate reprimand from whatever adult witnessed our misbehavior, and our parents often heard about it before we got home. We knew what our limits were, and although we sometimes pushed those limits, we seldom exceeded them. We realized that our good conduct insured our freedom.

My brother Jerry loved to wander around town. If a hunting party was being formed, Jerry attached himself, so for his tenth birthday, Mother bought him a hunting rifle. When a neighbor commented on his being a bit young for a real rifle, Mother replied that since he was determined to follow the hunters, he might as well be properly equipped.

Hunting was exciting, but the most interesting activities were found along the railroad tracks. In fact, when Jerry was twelve, the railroad yards became an amusement park for him and his friends. One irresistible attraction was the stash of railroad torpedoes stored in boxes along the side of the train tracks that led into town. The torpedoes were small devices about two inches square, covered in red paper. They had the explosive equivalent of a fourth of a stick of dynamite. At the first sign of trouble along the rail line, such as another train stranded on the tracks ahead, railroad flagmen strapped torpedoes to the rails. When the wheels of the oncoming engine ran over them, they exploded with a loud boom, warning the engineer to proceed no farther.

Jerry and his pals used to open the storage boxes and help themselves to a few of the torpedoes, taking care to leave most of them in case of a rail emergency. They attached the torpedoes to a rail spur upon which the railroad employees had parked a hand-propelled pump car. Two of the boys would mount and, with a see-sawing motion, propel the pump car along the spur. The bang as the wheels of the pump car ran over one or more of the torpedoes was as satisfying to the boys as the explosion of a giant firecracker.

One game of skill the boys enjoyed was to stand on "The Hump" and wait for a train to come down the track. The Hump was an elevated bridge, part of the Old Cape Charles Road that led over the tracks toward the cemetery, the colored elementary school, and the Government Dock. The boys had an ongoing competition that involved tallying how many stones each boy could toss from the top of the hump into the smokestacks of trains when they passed below.

One summer day in 1954, when Jerry was twelve, he and his classmates, L. T. Bradford, Preston Lewis, Bobby Steffens and his older brother Charles, and Bond Disharoom were sitting on the beach. Looking toward the railroad complex, they speculated how it would feel to jump from the roof of the Pennsylvania Railroad's coal chute tower into the town's harbor. The soot-blackened tower stood several stories high above the harbor, and served as the fuel replenishment site for the railroad's tugboats. The top part of the tower consisted of a coal storage shed supported on four legs, with a roof that slanted down toward the ferry channel. A conveyer belt brought coal to the top of the shed and loaded it into the shed through a hatch. Boats needing to be refueled pulled up under the tower, from which a chute dropped down to deposit coal into the engine's tender.

The boys walked from the beach and crossed the vacant lot where the firemen held their annual carnival. They moved along the railroad's property to the inner harbor. Since the ferries had recently moved from Cape Charles to a new terminal at Kiptopeke Beach, eight miles away, there were few people around the harbor to observe the boy's antics. The tugboats, however, continued pulling their barges across the Bay from Cape Charles to Norfolk and Little Creek.

When they were sure that they could approach the coal chute without being noticed, the boys hurried to climb up the ladder on the outside of the tower. They crawled through the doorway of the chute. Once inside, they mounted another ladder that led to the hatch, and pulled themselves up through the hatch onto the roof.

Wow! The coal chute was formidably higher than the diving board at the beach. Should they really go ahead and jump? If so, who would go first? Charles Steffens, having jumped from the coal chute in previous summers, volunteered. He ran down the slanting roof and leapt off the edge. The long fall landed him deeply into the channel. As he surfaced, he saw L. T. in midair. Then the other boys hurled themselves into the void. They felt the shock of hitting the cold water, followed by a steady rise to the surface. How they laughed! How exhilarating to have accomplished such a feat!

From time to time, the boys treated themselves to the thrill of jumping off the coal chute. They reminded each other to use the sailor's dive to counteract the force with which they hit the water from such a great height. *Don't forget to keep your arms at your side and both legs tightly together. As soon as you hit the water, start back up so you won't go too deep.* Jerry always said that jumping off the tower was one way to find out if your bathing suit was any good. "When you came down like a cannonball and hit the water hard, the back of your bathing suit could split."

The friends were not unobserved. The railroad detective was aware of their antics and, whenever he caught sight of them leaping off the tower, he would yell, "Get down from that tower. I know who you are. I know who your fathers are, and I'm going to report you." Fortunately, he never did.

The railroad roundhouse, where the direction of the locomotives was reversed on a giant turntable, and the shops where trains were maintained were among the busiest centers in town. The boys could casually walk into the roundhouse, and then move on to the shops to observe welders, blacksmiths, carpenters, electricians, machinists, and the tinsmith at work. The workers kept to their tasks and, as long as the youngsters stayed out of the way, they did not object to the boys' visits.

At a spur in the yards, the railroad's boxcars were joined together in an operation called "humping." A locomotive would push a boxcar up a little rise. When the engineer released the boxcar, it shot down the rise until it slammed into the end of one of the cars on the lower end of the track, attaching the two boxcars.

Inside the boxcars, highly polished oak floors suggested an activity that the boys called "boxcar riding." They each took a cardboard box into a boxcar during the humping operation. Sitting in their boxes at the higher end of the boxcar, they waited for the engineer to release it. Once released, the boxcar slammed into the car below. As if shot from a slingshot, the boys in their cardboard boxes zipped across the slick floor toward the other end of the boxcar. Then they grabbed their boxes, jumped out, and waited to climb into the next boxcar to be coupled. The engineer always played along with them, as if he enjoyed the fun he was providing. Had he gone boxcar riding, himself, when he was young?

Unloading the morning's catch at Edgerton's packing shed

STINGRAYS AND CLAMS

A large ice plant stood along the railroad tracks at the end of Fig Street, near Route 13. It provided ice for the railroad's freight cars and for long-haul refrigerated trucks. Ice was produced when water was poured into five-by-two-foot vats and frozen into five-hundred-pound blocks. Jerry and his friends loved to go to the ice plant, inhale the musty smell of the air inside, and slide across the frozen vats of ice.

Edgerton's seafood brokerage and processing plant was located nearby, at the inner end of Cape Charles harbor. One side of its long shed-like building was an open dock where the watermen from whom Mr. Edgerton bought seafood unloaded their catch. Jerry and his pals were attracted by the activity generated at Edgerton's Seafood when crabs were being processed. They watched as containers of crabs were lowered into steam vats. A few minutes later, the steamed crabs were brought up, dumped onto belts, and conveyed to long tables where women picked and packed them for shipping. The boys loved to walk through the busy packing shed and observe as cans of crab moved quickly down conveyer belts. They listened to the sound of the pickers' chatter, breathed in the smell of the prepared crabmeat, and were fascinated to see how the crabs' shells turned from blue to orange after they had been cooked.

Whenever conch was being prepared for shipping, the friends staggered through the packing shed clutching their throats, choking and gagging in an exaggerated manner to express their dislike for the unpleasant odor conch emits during cooking. The women on the packing line warned them not to make fun of the smell. Didn't they know that bubble gum was made from conch?

If they were hungry—and they always were—each boy would pick up a couple of the steamed crabs as he passed by the tables. None of Edgerton's pickers paid the least bit of attention. They just went on with their work. What were a few crabs among the many that were swimming all around us in the Bay? Sitting on the dock at Edgerton's Seafood, Jerry and his friends feasted on the succulent white crab meat as they gazed out across the water.

The ice plant had a machine shop designed to keep the company's equipment in good working order. The boys liked to slip into the shop and watch the machinists and blacksmiths at work. When the men in the machine shop heard the boys talking about their visits to the seafood plant, they suggested a way in which the youngsters might be able to earn some money.

In the course of conducting business at the ice plant, Mr. Edgerton had complained to the employees that stingrays were ruining his clam beds by digging into the sand and eating the clams. He had mentioned that he would pay one dollar each for any stingrays brought to him from those that were attacking his clam beds.

A dollar a stingray? The boys were excited at the money-making potential. They said they would be happy to hunt down those predators, so the men at the machine shop fashioned metal spears that the boys could attach to wooden poles and use to spike the stingrays. Armed with their spears, the boys got to work. And, sure enough, Mr. Edgerton did pay a dollar for each stingray.

After spearing stingrays for a couple of weeks, the boys came up with a better idea. *Why not also dig up some of the clams and sell them to Edgerton's Seafood?* The first day they brought Mr. Edgerton a bushel of clams from his beds, he gave them a penny a clam. All summer, the boys worked in the hot sun, digging clams for a penny each. At the end of the season, Mr. Edgerton told them that he did not need any more clams. He thanked them for their hard work and said how much he appreciated it. "After all, it would have cost me a nickel apiece to have them harvested. You kids thought that you were pulling a fast one, stealing my clams and selling them back to me. Let this be a lesson—you could have earned five times the money, if only you had asked."

Thanksgiving, 1954

Besides being a provider of education for young people from first through twelfth grade, Cape Charles High School served to bring the community together in various ways. One major event was the annual Thanksgiving Day football game between the Northampton High School Yellow Jackets and the Cape Charles Indians. In 1954, it would be held at Cape Charles, as Northampton High School had hosted the game the year before.

The Cape Charles/Northampton football game was not just a school event, but a homecoming for the entire community. Many adults who lived in the town and county attended, whether they had or did not have children in school. College students home for the holiday and former residents who had left to find work elsewhere all returned to the Eastern Shore to celebrate Thanksgiving with relatives.

1954 had not been a good year for the community. The last ferry running from Cape Charles, our much-loved SS *Elisha Lee* had made her final trip across the Bay the year before, despite vehement protests from the town's citizens. This left Cape Charles with no direct passenger link to Norfolk or Little Creek. Route 13 had been rerouted to bypass Cape Charles in order to serve the new ferry terminal at Kiptopeke Beach. Now in '54, the Pennsylvania Railroad was ripping up one of the two railroad tracks that served the area—another brutal manifestation of the town's fading economy.

1954 had not been a good season for the Cape Charles High

School Indians, either. The smallest high school on the Eastern Shore, with a team of only twelve players, they had lost to the larger teams from the county schools as well as to Norfolk Academy. The Matthews County High School team had crossed the Bay in fishing boats. We lost to them, too. Our team ended this devastating losing streak with one of its players injured and unable to play in the Thanksgiving game. We would be meeting the big Northampton High School team with only eleven players. Predictions favored the Yellow Jackets winning by fourteen points. After all, they had beaten the Cape Charles Indians with a score of nineteen to zero the previous year.

I would not dream of missing the pep rally and bonfire that took place on the school grounds the night before a game. All the high school students, bundled in jackets against the autumn chill, gathered around the bonfire. The crackle and fragrance of the burning wood and spitting sparks added an element of excitement that the fire's eye-stinging smoke could not dampen. Cheerleaders in heavy white sweaters, maroon circle skirts, and saddle shoes energetically performed to whip up school spirit. Wisely, the teachers and coaches stood in the background away from the smoke, until the captain of the football team and the coaches stepped forward with speeches intended to inspire the team to pursue victory on the field and the spectators to rah, rah them on with gusto from the sidelines.

After the pep rally, Jane, Jerry, and I walked home in the dark. Faces still flushed from the heat of the fire, we chatted about what the next day might bring. Jane kept repeating that our team would win, but I argued that, since our school had lost every game it had played all season, the chances that we would beat the Northampton Yellow Jackets were not good. I reminded her that we had only eleven players. It would take a miracle.

The next morning, our house was redolent of the baking turkey that had been stuffed and slipped into the oven in the very early hours. A holiday aroma of celery, onion, cinnamon, and sage heralded a traditional Thanksgiving dinner. Jane and I set the dining room table with Mother's best china, the china that was only used on Sundays and holidays, and which always promised a festive meal.

Kickoff was scheduled for noon, in order to leave time for family gatherings later in the day. Jane and I dressed with care in our fall suits, nylon stockings, and dress pumps, as both of us were to be part of the homecoming queen's float. We walked out into the crisp autumn air, to the school grounds. Northampton High School had two floats already in place: one with a throne for their football queen, and another displaying a giant yellow jacket chasing an Indian out of a full-size teepee. Our float was smaller, containing only the throne for the football queen, whom the team had chosen by secret ballot and whose name would be revealed at halftime. The cheerleaders and the more enthusiastic spectators sported big yellow chrysanthemum pompoms tied up with ribbons and streamers of maroon and gold, Cape Charles' school colors.

Neither team scored during the first two quarters. At halftime, as we prepared to climb onto the school float, Jane nudged me in the ribs, "Have you noticed? Northampton hasn't made a touchdown." As soon as all who were taking part in the halftime ceremonies were in their places, the Northampton High School band led the lumbering floats onto the field. Convertibles filled with cheerleaders and decorated in the schools' colors followed. After they had paraded a bit, the cheerleaders had performed, and the band had played its school song, it was time to crown the football queens. I was delighted to find that the Cape Charles team had chosen me as queen. Then, ceremonies over, we spent the rest of halftime with our friends and families on the sidelines. The Cape Charles fans were thrilled and amazed that their team had actually kept Northampton from scoring during the entire first half.

Alas, to the despair of the Cape Charles Indians, the Yellow Jackets made a touchdown in the third quarter, giving them six points. Then, as reported in the *Northampton Times*:

> Trailing 6–0 in the fourth and final period the fighting Indians started their drive to paydirt from their own 31 yard line. Led by quarterback Keith Pusey the Indians

combined six first downs in succession to place the ball on the Northampton two yard line. Then a holding penalty by a Cape Charles lineman returned the ball to the 17 yard line. This infraction at the time seemed to be the coup de grace. With less than two minutes remaining it appeared that the boys from 'up the road' had not only copped the dressing but the Thanksgiving turkey as well. . . .

In the last few seconds of the game, Gary White made the tying touchdown, and though the try for the extra point failed, the Cape Charles fans whooped with enthusiasm, as thrilled as if our team had won the game. After the game, Jane, the family's optimist, couldn't resist interjecting, "Told you so!" as our family discussed the miracle that had taken place before our eyes.

We returned home to a comforting meal of turkey, stuffing, mashed potatoes, gravy, green beans, turnip or collard greens, sweet potatoes, cranberry sauce, and a relish tray of celery, carrot sticks, olives, and pickles. Of course, there was pumpkin pie for dessert.

Beyond the Salt Marsh

Residents of the Eastern Shore of Virginia refer to their homes as being on either the "bayside" or the "seaside" of the Delmarva Peninsula. It depends upon whether one's community or farm lies on the Chesapeake Bay side of Route 13, or on the Atlantic Ocean side. The seaside of the peninsula is protected from the heavy surf of the Atlantic Ocean by a chain of barrier islands. Of this chain of fourteen islands, only Assateague Island has a bridge to the peninsula. The rest are accessible by boat, or occasionally by air.

When I was sixteen, I had a boyfriend, Kenneth, who lived across an inlet from the seaside village of Oyster, a few miles northeast of Cape Charles. He was a genuinely kind person, fun to be with, and I was very fond of him; but somehow, our outings often had a hair-raising element or else produced an uncomfortable result. Sometimes, Kenneth would meet me after school and, with a group of teenage hangers-on, he would drive us to the Cape Center at Kiptopeke for hamburgers and fries. On Saturday evenings, we might see a movie at the Palace or Radium Theatre. Those were normal dates. The problem was that we just couldn't stay away from the water—whether it was enjoying a romantic trip up one of the Chesapeake Bay inlets in Kenneth's outboard motorboat, taking his father's fishing vessel out to the ocean, or visiting the numerous piers and docks that served the bayside and seaside communities.

Kenneth's father, Captain Doughty, fished for a living, and Kenneth's brother was a seafood broker. Occasionally, on weekends, Kenneth borrowed his father's workboat and invited me and a few of our friends for a day of fishing off Cobb Island Light. We would leave Oyster Slip in the early morning. Kenneth would guide the boat out to the ocean by following a channel that wove its way through the salt marsh. Miles of marshland displaying a rich variety of sea grasses opened up before us. The salt marshes teemed with many species of birds. It seemed as if there was no end to the types of ducks that rose from the marsh as we approached. Sometimes we were fortunate enough to see one or more of the stately great blue herons standing by a pool within the marsh.

Kenneth admitted that he was happiest out on the water. He once told me that when he fished with his father and crew, he felt so lighthearted that he would start singing. In fact, he taught himself to yodel as he worked in his father's boat. I understood. Whenever I was offshore on a good day, nature seemed fresh and new, as if the surface of the water, the sky, and the clouds had been swept clean by the brisk ocean air. Just being in such an immense space made me feel free, untroubled, and invigorated.

One Sunday, Kenneth invited me, along with my sister Jane and a few of our friends, to go fishing. By then I had learned how to follow the channel out to the ocean, and I must have insisted, because Kenneth let me take the wheel of the boat while he busied himself preparing our tackle and bait. (What would Captain Doughty have said, had he known?) Well supplied with bait and fishing poles, we spent the day happily casting our lines into the depths off the base of Cobb Island Light. There were quite a few fishing charters all around us. Though we patiently tended our fishing poles, we only hooked a few small fish, which we threw back. A fishing party anchored nearby was busy drinking beer and pulling in hefty bass or drum, while others in the same area were catching nothing. On the way back to shore, Jane complained that the only thing she had caught was "a bad sunburn."

As soon as we returned to Cape Charles, Jane and I hurried to change into our white dresses. We were to perform with the glee club at the high school's baccalaureate ceremony. That evening in the high school auditorium, surrounded by all the girls in white, I imagined that my face, like the faces of those who had been part of the fishing party, stood out like a red hot chili pepper.

Kenneth's ancestors had settled on one of the barrier islands, Hog Island, in the 1700s. For over a hundred and fifty years, they supported themselves by fishing, hunting, and harvesting oysters. Generations later, the island started to wash away. During the 1930s hurricanes, it became flooded, and much of the island disappeared, reclaimed by the ocean. When the island town of Broadwater was wiped out, the islanders moved their houses by barge to the villages of Willis Wharf, Oyster, and other seaside towns. Once a year, descendants of the families that had to abandon their island community held an annual reunion on what remained of Hog Island.

The summer that Kenneth was nineteen years old, his parents, along with the parents of one of Kenneth's cousins, planned to attend the reunion. Kenneth invited me to go with them. He picked me up for our date early in the morning, and I met his parents for the first time on the dock in Oyster. Eager to please Kenneth's mother, I helped load the supplies for the day's outing. An aroma of fried chicken seeped from the ladies' picnic baskets and hung in the air. Then both ladies stepped on board, each bearing a freshly baked, lavishly iced layer cake.

As we were heading through the channel to the ocean, Kenneth and his cousin announced that they did not want to go to the reunion after all. The reunion would only be a lot of people talking about folks who had passed away years ago, and they had heard those stories many times. Kenneth made a suggestion. If we younger people could be left on one of the sandbars that appear near the barrier islands when the tide is out, we could dig for clams without being accused of poaching on clam beds that might be leased to others.

I wasn't sure that I preferred clamming to picnicking. I could dig for clams on the public beach in Cape Charles anytime. But since it was Kenneth who had invited me to come on the expedition, I did not feel that it was my place to object. The Doughtys tried to dissuade us, but finally agreed to the clamming project.

Captain Doughty brought the boat in close to a selected site. Clutching the boat's buckets, we jumped overboard and waded onto the sandbar as the adults pushed off on their way to Hog Island. What a disappointment! I wanted to see Hog Island. I was looking forward to hearing the tales of hardship and danger that nature had wrought upon the hearty islanders, and about how those old island families had survived over the centuries. Besides, the thought of attending a well-provisioned picnic, sitting in the shade, and enjoying an ocean breeze was my idea of a pleasant afternoon.

We roamed the sandbar, kidding each other, competing as we looked for the small holes that indicated the presence of clams under the sand. They were so plentiful that, digging into the pungent-smelling grey silt below, we soon brought up enough to fill three large buckets. Then there was nothing to do but wait to be picked up and taken back to dry land. As the day progressed, our conversation waned. I regretted missing out on the contents of Mrs. Doughty's picnic baskets, and imagined what savory potato salad, Southern fried chicken, biscuits with country ham, and succulent peaches might have nestled within—and just the thought of the beautiful homemade cakes that had sailed away to Hog Island. Oh, my!

The day seemed to go on forever. Late in the afternoon, concerned that the tide might soon rise, I started scanning the horizon—but there was no boat in sight. I wanted to scream at Kenneth, blaming him because I was now intensely hungry, achingly tired, and admittedly scared. I could see that he looked worried, so I tried to appear cheerful, but my anxiety became paralysis when I heard an uneasy rustling sound as the tide started to turn. I knew that the sandbar would eventually be deeply submerged. Indeed, it seemed to be getting smaller. I could only think that we had been forgotten and would soon drown. What if the Doughtys came too late and found that we had been swept out to sea? Evening approached. The water was rising almost to our ankles. At last, heavenly relief—we saw the boat. We were rescued!

As I pulled myself on board, I felt a twinge of resentment toward the Doughtys for the anxiety I had experienced. Had they purposely delayed their arrival as punishment for our disdaining to attend the Hog Island reunion? Of course not. I realize now that Kenneth's parents had to shorten their visit to Hog Island in order to pluck us off the sandbar before it became inundated.

I've never cared to dig clams since, and will turn down any invitation to do so—but I will always be grateful to Kenneth for introducing me, a bayside girl, to the wild beauty of the salt marshes on the ocean side of our Eastern Shore peninsula.

Palace Theater, an Art Deco treasure

In Pursuit of Fashion

A weekly newspaper, the *Northampton Times*, was published in Cape Charles. It gave limited coverage to world and national news; readers could obtain all that information elsewhere. The important news was local. Articles suggested planting times, told of innovations in the science of farming, gave tips on how to care for poultry, and presented other information of importance to farmers. Reports about the abundance of oysters or fish interested workers in the seafood industry. Readers looked to see if their names were mentioned among news items covering the local schools, clubs, and civic organizations. The Society section described weddings and social events in great detail, as well as any awards or honors Northampton County residents received. "Personals" columns for each Northampton County community filled most of the paper, and kept citizens informed of the visits back and forth of their friends and neighbors.

For all these social activities, the participants needed to be well turned-out, even for their trips to Norfolk. And indeed, though many of us made the occasional Bay crossing to Norfolk to shop, we had ample shopping opportunities right here on the Eastern Shore.

Each week for many years, advertisements by two competing department stores covered a goodly portion of an inside page of the *Northampton Times*. On the left side of the page, Wilson's of Cape Charles directed the reader's attention to their recent shipments of housewares and fashions. On the right side, Benjamin's of Exmore, twenty miles north of Cape Charles, advertised its latest styles with an equally large ad. Wilson's was, by far, the biggest store on the Eastern Shore of Virginia, but Benjamin's, its worthy rival, carried an excellent selection of clothing. Year in and year out, these two competitors maintained beachheads on the same pages in the *Northampton Times*.

In the fall of 1952, my sister Jane, Ellen Bradford, a fourth girl, and I took the bus to Exmore to buy new dresses to wear to a dance. Benjamin's was located at a point on Route 13 in such a way that the entrance to the store was practically on the highway. When the bus doors opened to let us off in front of Benjamin's, we jumped down onto the curb and ran up a flight of stairs that led from the street into a veritable Aladdin's cave of new fashions—fashions that the other girls in Cape Charles, who only investigated Wilson's stock, were unlikely to have seen. We happily spent the afternoon at Benjamin's, trying on one dress after another, laughing, and joking, while opinions as to the suitability of this or that dress flew freely from person to person. By the time we had finalized and paid for our choices and the saleswoman had carefully boxed them up, it was after five o'clock. We had missed the last bus back to Cape Charles.

We spent half an hour calling friends and families from the telephone booth across the street from Benjamin's. It was fruitless. Where was everyone? Was there no one who could drive us back to town? Our only option was to start walking.

Lugging our shopping bags, we had walked a mile out of Exmore along Route 13 when, chances being good that someone we knew would come along, we decided that we would have to start thumbing for a ride. Otherwise, before long, we would be hiking down the highway in the dark. What a strange sight it must have been to see four stylishly dressed teenage girls lugging large packages as they bummed rides along the highway.

Happily, two airmen driving back to Cape Charles Air Force Station soon recognized us as residents of Cape Charles and picked us up. We gratefully squeezed our crinoline-skirted selves and those of our bulky packages that did not fit in the trunk of the car into the backseat of the sedan. At that time of our lives, we thought everything was funny, and—the relief of being off the highway making us more jocular than usual—we continued our joking and laughing throughout the uncomfortable twenty-mile ride back to Cape Charles. I'm sure that when we got to Cape Charles, the airmen were happy to be relieved of such exuberant passengers.

As fundraisers for civic causes, Wilson's and Benjamin's sometimes held fashion shows at the Palace Theatre or, occasionally, in the high school auditorium. These shows, featuring men's fashions along with those of women and children, were always well attended. Jane modeled in many of them, and I modeled in a few as well. But it was apparent that I did not have the stage presence of a model. Years before, when I was eleven, I had disgraced myself as an entrant in a talent show that was being held at the Palace Theatre, by having to be coaxed onto the stage. On the other hand, Jane, dressed in a straw hat and denim overalls, won second place for her rendition of "Sioux City Sue." She was fearless in front of an audience.

When I was a junior in high school, Benjamin's Department Store planned a fashion show that included styles of yesteryear. Most of the "yesteryear" fashions were not costumes, but actual clothes from the late nineteenth century. Sponsors of the fashion show had invited some of the girls from our school to be models. I, with my awkward way of walking and my retiring personality, did not receive the compliment of being asked.

The most stunning garment in that show was to be a wedding gown of heavy white lace, only slightly yellowed—a family heirloom that belonged to my friend Catherine Lambertson's grandmother, Mrs. Wendell. The gown appeared to be from the 1880s, with its high collar, tiny waistline, and tight sleeves. The narrow skirt fell in one straight piece in front, and at the back, it was gathered up into a bustle with a short train. But there was a problem: none of the models could get into the dress; and, being an antique garment that required careful handling, it could not be altered.

By the time of dress rehearsal, no one had found a model for the wedding gown. Then someone suggested calling on me, because I was so thin. Though I realized that I was there as an afterthought, I attended the final fitting and tried on the gown. It fit perfectly, and I didn't look too thin at all. What a fuss the show's sponsors made over me! They treated me as if I was a hero coming to their rescue.

The night of the show, the old-fashioned wedding gown was the last item on the program. When my turn came to go on, someone thrust a white lace parasol into my hand, and, confident that the gown would be a show stopper, I stepped onto the stage. "For Me and My Gal," a popular song from 1917 that had been resurrected in a 1940s movie of the same name, was the background theme for my dress. I floated down the runway to the rhythm of the music. Where there was a pause in the music, I paused. I could feel that my delight in presenting such a beautifully designed garment had communicated itself to the audience. Murmurs of approval sounded throughout the theatre. I even heard someone exclaim that I was beautiful! I left the stage to hearty applause, and although I was tempted, I am proud that once backstage, I did not stick my tongue out at the other models.

A few years later, a Mr. Parry and his mother opened a small dress shop on Strawberry Street. They carried a line of stylish dresses of good quality. Before opening his shop, Mr. Parry had been in charge of one of the clothing departments on the mezzanine at Wilson's. After the passenger trains stopped running from Cape Charles and the ferries moved away in the mid-1950s, Wilson's business, like other businesses in Cape Charles, began to decline. Mr. Parry and his mother, suspecting that Wilson's might have to close, decided to open their own clothing store.

The Parrys often called on Jane and me to model their clothing. At one of their fashion shows, Jane fell in love with a low-backed black sheath dress made of a heavyweight low-sheen satin that she had worn in the show. That evening at the dinner table, she told us how much she loved and wanted the dress, but Mother said she could not buy it for her. The next afternoon, when Jane came home from cheerleading practice, behold: there, lying across her bed, was the black satin dress. Delighted, she ran downstairs to thank Mother.

"James is the one you should thank," Mother replied. She explained how James, our twelve-year-old brother, had walked into Parry's dress shop that afternoon and asked the Parrys which black dress Jane had modeled. Then, with the money he had saved from his after-school job of delivering groceries, he paid for the dress. Jane was thrilled at first—but immediately afterward, she felt guilty that her desire to make a fashion statement had prompted her younger brother to spend the hard-earned money he had been saving. She begged him to take the dress back to the Parrys, but he refused. She thought of returning it herself until, reflecting upon how much the gift expressed James' sincere wish for her happiness, she let the matter drop.

The summer between my freshman and sophomore years at college, retailers launched a new fashion item in casual wear: Bermuda shorts. Toward the end of September, I made the ferry trip from Kiptopeke to Norfolk to shop. Smith and Welton's Department Store had an attractive display of its fall line of wool and corduroy "Bermudas," as those shorts were called. Interested in being on the forefront of fashion, I bought a pair of corduroy Bermudas in the Black Watch tartan and a pair of navy blue kneesocks.

While I was returning home, a strong wind arose, and the water on the Bay became choppy. That evening, rain poured down, and for several days we kept indoors, out of the nor'easter.

After the rain ceased, I decided to do a final shopping for my return to school. I felt very avant-garde as I dressed to go downtown. At last I had an opportunity to wear my new Bermuda shorts and knee socks. As far as I knew, no one else had tried to initiate this fashion in Cape Charles. Pushing through the wind, I walked the several blocks to Mason Avenue under a low grey sky to pick up the few items I wanted to pack for the trip back to school.

A break in the weather had brought many people onto the streets. I noticed some of them looked at me and my costume with astonished expressions, and their glances were more of shock than of admiration. I was wishing I hadn't been so quick to spring the

Bermudas on the townspeople of Cape Charles, whom I, in my youthful arrogance, considered to be behind the times. I took some comfort in remembering that I had been the first to sport Capri pants when they came into vogue. Everyone thought the Capris odd at first, but soon most of the younger women in town owned a pair or two.

As often happened during a storm, fishing fleets could be stranded in Cape Charles while they waited out the heavy weather. During the nor'easter, a fleet of fishing boats from Tangier Island had anchored in the relative calm of the harbor. With nothing to do until it was safe to leave, the watermen roamed around town, trying out the playground equipment at the school and taking in the sights. That afternoon, a row of about ten Tangier watermen were sitting on the pavement on Mason Avenue, their backs resting against the walls of the storefronts. In their distinctive dialect, they made frank and audible comments on all who passed by. When I came into view with my bare knees on display, I certainly got their attention. They mocked my Bermudas and, through their laughter, I could hear phrases like "What is that? I never seen nothin' like that," all loudly expressed in their inimitable Tangier Island accents. My face burned with embarrassment. Then, to comfort myself, I thought, *Let them laugh. Such hardworking men deserve some amusement. And after all, why should I expect men who live on an isolated island in the Chesapeake Bay to be up to date on this year's latest styles?*

THE NORFOLK AND WESTERN RAILROAD

Three of us who had graduated from Cape Charles High School stepped into the *Powhatan Arrow*, Norfolk and Western's morning train heading west from Norfolk. It was October of 1956. Roger Lee Navarro was entering his first year at Virginia Polytechnic Institute, and Jennie Buchanan and I were going into the freshman class at nearby Radford College. At that time, "Virginia Tech" (as Virginia Polytechnic Institute was commonly called) was a military school, and Radford College was the women's division of Virginia Tech. Roger Lee was eager to begin his engineering studies; Jennie wanted to be a lab technician; and as for me, I had no idea what I wanted to do. Roger Lee went on to work for NASA at Wallops Island after graduation; Jennie did become a lab technician; and I never did find out what I wanted to do.

We were traveling to Norfolk by ferry, having left Cape Charles just as dawn was breaking. We had taken a ride to the Kiptopeke ferry terminal, then a trip of one hour and twenty minutes across the Chesapeake Bay to Norfolk. Somehow we got ourselves to the Norfolk and Western train station to catch the morning train going west.

After seeing our trunks loaded safely into the baggage car, we stepped into the coach of the *Powhatan Arrow*—but since the train was crowded, we could not sit together, so we moved to the observation car. It was a good move, as the seats in the car were roomy and comfortable.

The only other passenger in the observation car was a middle-aged man in business attire who was traveling on to Cincinnati. The gentleman asked us where we were going. We introduced ourselves and told him our destination. He asked Roger Lee if he was related to a count he knew named Navarro. The gentleman must have traveled in high circles, unlike Roger Lee, who confessed that he had no relatives among European nobility.

A white-jacketed waiter was assigned to the observation car. We ordered glasses of ginger ale and, later, sandwiches.

We soon left the flat country to which we were accustomed. How glorious it was to see the changing terrain and evidence of the changing season, as the leaves on the mountains began to change color, unlike the evergreens that surrounded us on the Eastern Shore. Late in the afternoon, Jennie and I arrived in Radford, and Roger Lee traveled on to Blacksburg.

The trip between Radford and Cape Charles was so long that we never attempted to travel home for the relatively short Thanksgiving or Easter breaks. Instead, we were often hosted by parents of other students who lived nearby and who felt sorry for our having to celebrate the holidays so far from our families. My only trip home during freshman year was for Christmas break. The Norfolk and Western left Radford in the late afternoon. When it arrived in Roanoke, there was a long layover, so I left the train and walked across the tracks to the luxurious railroad hotel, the Hotel Roanoke. In the comfort and elegance of the dining room with its white tablecloths, soft carpet, and elegant lighting, I was tempted to "go all out," so I ordered an expensive seafood dinner that I told myself I deserved, since I would be sitting up all night on the train.

Classes began on January second after Christmas break; so, early on New Year's Day, my mother and I took the ferry across the Bay to Norfolk. We spent the afternoon at the Kellams' home, visiting with them and the Post family, our neighbors from Cape Charles, who had moved away when the ferries and the railroad left and the town began to decline. Like many railroad employees who found themselves unemployed, Mr. Kellam and Mr. Post were able to transfer their expertise to jobs at the Norfolk Naval Shipyard. My mother was delighted to see her old friends once more. We caught up on all that had been happening in each family's lives while they plied us with sandwiches, fruitcake, and tea.

When it was time to catch the train back to Radford, Mrs. Post, the Kellams, and their adolescent daughters Patricia Kellam and Trudy Post came with us to the station to see me off. Around ten o'clock in the evening, the passengers gathered on the platform while they waited to board the *Cavalier*. They were mostly students, many in party dresses or their best suits, for they had come straight from their holiday festivities to catch the train. Shortly after ten, I waved to Mother and our old neighbors as the train pulled out of the station.

Around midnight, the *Cavalier* chugged into the town of Petersburg, Virginia, where there was a layover. The conductor announced that the café in the old Petersburg train station would be open. The station was immediately crowded with students. Facing a long overnight trip, I decided to fortify myself with a sandwich. I was waiting for my order to be prepared when I heard someone calling out, "What's your name?"

I looked toward the end of the counter, and again: "What's your name?" A tall young man whom I had never met was looking at me.

He moved up the counter to stand next to me. "Are you at Radford?"

I told him that I was indeed going to Radford. He asked my name and the phone number of my dorm. When I hesitated, he went on to explain, "I go to Tech, and all of us cadets are required to attend the big cotillion next month. If we don't already have a date, one will be assigned to us by lottery, and I don't want to get stuck."

He introduced himself as Drexel Bradshaw, and since he was good-looking, I gave him the phone number of the pay phone on the second floor of my dormitory. After all, it was also mandatory that the Radford girls attend the cotillion, and without a date, my name would have been on the lottery list. I didn't want to get "stuck" either.

After we got back on the train, his equally good-looking friend Ed Darden also asked if I had a date for the dance, but I told him that I had already promised Drex. I felt rich indeed, having met two possible dates for future dances.

After the Petersburg layover, the dreaded train ride became lively, with students visiting back and forth, standing in the aisles, planning dates, and chatting until around two in the morning. Then exhaustion kicked in, and silence fell upon the passenger car until we arrived in Radford in the early morning.

The cotillion turned out to be great fun. The Radford girls were taken from our campus to Virginia Tech in chartered buses. The evening gowns of that era featured big wide skirts, making it hard to squeeze ourselves down the aisle of the bus and into our seats. After we arrived at Tech and attempted to straighten out our crumpled gowns, we made our way into the grey stone building where the dance was being held. The cadets were lined up in formation. In the days before the dance, our class advisors had given each girl a card with the name of her date and the company to which he belonged. After we located our date's company, we presented the card to his company's commander and he called out our date's name. The cadet whose name was called stepped out of formation and then escorted his date onto the dance floor. It was all extremely formal.

To add to the old-fashioned atmosphere, each girl had a dance card, a little booklet with a small pencil attached by a cord, which she tied to her white-gloved wrist, and in which the young men who wished to dance with her wrote their names. Most of us had names written in our dance card for the first two or three dances; after that, we became less formal and either stuck with our dates, or not. I certainly stuck with mine—the one I had met in the train station in Petersburg.

THE TROWER FAMILY

Mandy, if you would give me your address, my husband can come to get you on bad days and you won't have to walk here in the rain."

My mother picked up the dog-eared address book she kept on a table next to the hall telephone. As she prepared to take down Mandy's home address, Mandy reached for the book.

"Here," she said, "I can write it myself." She gently pulled the book from Mother's hand. Then, unhesitatingly, she added her address to the others on Mother's list.

"Why, Mandy, your handwriting is beautiful!" Mother said as she glanced at the address Mandy had written.

"Miz Trower taught me. See, everyt'ings edication over dere," Mandy replied. "Dat's all dey talk about, is edication." She was referring to the Trower family, with whom we shared Mandy's housekeeping services. She explained that when she started to work for the Trowers, Mrs. Alice Trower, a dedicated elementary school teacher, had been appalled that Mandy did not know how to read or write. Immediately, Mrs. Trower began to teach her. Mandy said that at first she had not been eager to spend her time practicing the Palmer writing method, with all of its repetition, and that she had found learning to read a tedious exercise. But now, she told Mother, she was glad that she was literate, and the ability to read the newspaper, besides being a source of pride for her, was one of her greatest pleasures.

Mandy's ancestors had been slaves of Dr. William Trower's ancestors, and though Mandy had a common-law husband, and another that she later married, she kept the name Trower. Mandy's grandmother had been one Henrietta Trower, and the name Trower had been passed down through the women in her family, as society in the ex-slave community on the Eastern Shore tended to be matriarchal.

Mrs. Alice Trower's daughter, Henrietta, was one of my close childhood friends. Once, when we were in our teens, Henrietta called a florist to order a corsage to wear to a special event. The florist inquired as to the color of her dress. When Henrietta told her, the florist said, "That dress will not go with your skin color." Henrietta insisted it would, but the florist suggested another set of colors. Finally Henrietta's mother got on the phone, and she and the florist figured out that Henrietta had called an African-American florist who thought she was talking to a different Henrietta Trower, a descendant of Mandy's grandmother. Of course, the skin tones were different. Names on the Eastern Shore could sometimes be confusing.

Mrs. Alice Trower taught sixth grade at Cape Charles High School. She had grown up the daughter of the keepers of Cape Charles Lighthouse on Smith Island, off the end of the Delmarva Peninsula. Her parents, the Duntons, as lighthouse keepers, had their housing provided, which was a great savings for the family. The lifestyle of lighthouse keepers, though sometimes lonely, enabled them to keep their living expenses small. They were able to save enough that they could afford to give their daughter an excellent education.

Mrs. Trower's husband, Dr. William Trower, was eighteen years older than his wife. He had served during World War I as the in-house physician at the Chamberlain Hotel at Old Point Comfort. He eventually gave up his practice to cultivate a family farm that he had inherited. The property included a section of Pickett's Harbor, an attractive beach several miles south of Cape Charles. Dr. Trower generously allowed the public to use the beach. He often descended the stairway that led down a cliff and onto the beach to check the fish nets he kept in the water. If anyone sprained an ankle or was cut by a piece of glass, he was quick to attend to the injury.

Every Friday after my father's death, Dr. Trower would bring our family fish from his nets. He cleaned and scaled the fish before he gave them, neatly wrapped in newspaper, to Mother. Our family appreciated the fish. Even more, we appreciated the trouble that Dr. Trower took to present them all ready to be cooked.

The Trowers had two daughters: Alice, who was a year older than I; and Henrietta, who was a year younger. Because they wanted the best for the girls, the Trowers were strict regarding their children's behavior, and because they didn't want them to pick up bad habits of speech or conduct, they were careful with whom they let them associate. Alice and Henrietta were rarely allowed to take part in after-school activities, and there was seldom a social event that their parents considered suitable for their daughters to attend. Instead they were encouraged to spend their time more profitably by following pursuits with educational benefits. This gave the parents the reputation of being snobbish, which was an unfair label for such a warm-hearted couple.

I was a friend of both girls but was especially close to Henrietta, who, being enterprising enough to slip through some of her parents' restrictions, was the more exciting companion. One summer when we were in high school, the Trower girls and I were invited to a clambake on one of the isolated beaches further up the peninsula. A group of college students who were home for the summer would be hosting. Since we thought it a compliment to be included in this older, more sophisticated crowd, we spent an afternoon discussing how best to ask our parents for permission to attend. First we approached my mother, who was slightly more liberal than Mrs. Trower. After I made many promises as to how I would conduct myself, she told me I could go. Then we went next door to try to obtain Mrs. Trower's permission. Mrs. Trower asked us several questions about the event while she thought the matter over. She hesitated for a while before she came to a decision. "Well, if Mrs. Joyce says that Patricia can go, then I think it's alright for you two to go." I was thrilled that we could all go to the clambake together, but I couldn't help feeling somewhat insulted that Mrs. Trower had determined the event must be tame indeed, if someone as strictly reared as I was allowed to attend.

The clambake turned out to be less exciting than we had expected. Sure, there was beer; but we did not have any. Our hosts provided a few clams, some potato chips, and hot dogs. There was a little desultory conversation here and there among the ten of us as we all sat on the sand and stared through the darkness and into the inky waters of the Chesapeake Bay—something Henrietta and I could have done from our own front porches.

The next morning, when I gave my mother a reassuring account of the clambake, she remarked that she had not been at all concerned. If Mrs. Trower approved of her daughters going, it would surely be suitable for me to attend. A realization struck me. This was how we could work on our parents. We had broken the code!

Several years later, when I was a college sophomore and it was time to return to school after Christmas vacation, I found myself short of funds with which to pay the second semester's tuition. I always saved for my tuition by working part-time at the telephone company during the Christmas and summer vacations. My father had been dead for three years, and Mother's widow's pension was stretched thin with three younger children at home, so funds were limited.

Henrietta and I were chatting in my backyard when Dr. Trower walked out of his kitchen door. He asked why I had not left for college. I told him I would not be attending this semester. When he questioned me further, I was embarrassed to confess that, because my employment over the Christmas vacation had been of short duration, I had not earned enough to pay my tuition. He asked how much I needed. I told him that I was one hundred and fifty dollars short. Immediately, he reached into his pocket, peeled off one hundred and fifty dollars from a wad of bills, and thrust them into my hand. I resisted, but he insisted.

Henrietta, having become overwhelmed by the curriculum she had been carrying, was hoping to expand her Christmas vacation for another semester. Over her objections, Dr. Trower demanded she also return to school. Mrs. Trower then put her car at our disposal, so we would not have to take the usual long bus and train trip, and would be at our schools in time to register. That very afternoon, Henrietta and I boarded the ferry at Kiptopeke Beach on our way back to face our scholastic endeavors.

Dance Lessons

On the Eastern Shore, the opportunity to attend a children's cotillion did not exist for my age group. Fortunately, my mother was a good dancer. She had been taught, in the era before the First World War, by an excellent dancer, and she taught me the classical ballroom dances she had learned.

As a child, Mother played with the children of the Nagy family, Hungarian immigrants who were trying to get started in this country and who lived in the alley behind her house. In her memoirs, my mother wrote:

> Mr. Nagy had been an officer in the Austrian army who, sensing war on the horizon, fled with his family to the United States using an assumed name, Nagy. This was a rumor, of course, but a splendid portrait of him in his pale blue uniform and medals hung in their parlor.... These were the first foreigners I had ever met and I was fascinated by them and their customs until soon my own home became little more than a sleeping place, I spent so much time with them.

In another section of her memoirs, Mother tells how, when she was a child, the Nagy family included her at a German singing society's picnic held on a farm near Pittsburgh, Pennsylvania:

A permanent dance floor occupied a wooded section, with picnic benches and tables surrounding it. Soon an orchestra appeared, from out of the woods, as far as I could see, and couples started dancing to a lovely waltz. I stood and stared. I could not get over my surprise at seeing a man and his wife dancing together, and enjoying it, too. Every once in a while, Mr. Nagy would throw his head back and laugh, while his wife smiled demurely at him, or the other dancers. He took his daughters out on the floor, in turn, swinging them around to the music. Their long beribboned plaits and starched petticoats swirled about them gracefully. Soon he was standing in front of me, hand outstretched. As I shrank back against the bench, he smiled. "Oh, no" I said, "I can't dance." "Now is the time for you to learn," he said, "I will teach you." So I had my first dancing lesson, one of many that he gave me along with his own children, and what a good teacher he was. I grew up to be an excellent dancer, to go to the college proms and tea dances of the twenties, and it all started on the dance floor at the German picnic.

Mother taught me the ballroom dances that had been in fashion when she was young. There was the schottische, foxtrot, and waltz, with emphasis on the waltz. I would waltz around the kitchen with my mother—"One-two-three, one-two-three, step-up-down, step-up-down"—until I became quite good at it.

When I was still in elementary school, my parents took me to watch some barn dances at the American Legion Hall. In those days, dances in Cape Charles usually began with the Virginia Reel, a nice communal sort of icebreaker with the men and women lined up facing each other as they might have in an English country dance in the early nineteenth century. In fact, the Virginia Reel was even taught to us at school, so that we would be prepared if we were invited to a dance. By the time I got to high school, the genteel Virginia Reel was no longer fashionable in Cape Charles. Rock and roll had arrived.

In my early teen years, I eagerly attended all the school dances that were held at the American Legion Hall, although I did not know how to do the new dances. Eager to join in the fun, I stood at the side of the hall, but I was never asked to dance. Some of the students had steady boyfriends and girlfriends, so they danced with each other. Some had older siblings who introduced them to the rock 'n' roll and swing that had come into vogue. The dances I had learned, which had been popular at the court of Emperor Franz Joseph, just didn't cut it anymore.

To add to my embarrassment at being the perennial wallflower, I felt uneasy because I knew that my father would be spending the evening in the lounge downstairs, waiting for our dance to end so he could drive me home. When I was sixteen, however, I acquired my own boyfriend, Kenneth Doughty, a handsome blond two years older than I. We were able to make it through the slow dances together.

By 1954, Kenneth and I had drifted apart. By that time, the US Army's Fort Custis at the tip of the Delmarva Peninsula had been turned over to the air force and was used as a radar station. Five hundred airmen were stationed there. That same year, I was introduced to several of the officers at the air force base, and over the next few years, they invited me to some social events at the BOQ, the bachelor officers' quarters.

The BOQ had a dimly lit lounge where we listened to modern progressive jazz and danced a little, but I always felt that the rhythms of progressive jazz lent themselves to very desultory dancing. Two or three times a month on a Saturday evening, the officers invited me to the BOQ, along with two girls from Cape Charles who had already graduated from college. I danced with our hosts and enjoyed myself somewhat, even though much of their conversation was over my head. Sometimes we would go out for the evening, usually to a restaurant or farther up the county to Silver Beach, where there was a place to buy beer and oysters and to dance. We always went as a group, and the older girls, Anne Lambertson and Anne Colonna, were unfailingly kind to me. I often wonder why I was included with this more mature company. Could there have been a shortage of young single women here in Northampton County, where so many girls married early?

One time, the enlisted men at the air force station sponsored a dance. Invitations were extended to girls from Cape Charles, Cheriton, and Eastville. My sister Jane and I attended. Unlike the officers, the enlisted men had been provided with a real dance hall on the base, which they had decorated with balloons and multicolored streamers. To our delight, the commanding officers had provided a live orchestra for the occasion, and it was playing the rock and roll songs that were popular with teenagers. Most of the enlisted men were quite young. Some were still in their teens in those days of compulsory military service. They were closer to my age than the officers I had been dating.

Although the hall was crowded with other girls, I danced every dance. How I enjoyed that evening—because by then, thanks to John Harlow, I had learned the current dances.

John was an airman who had grown up in Fond-du-Lac, Wisconsin and was now stationed at Cape Charles Air Force Station. He soon made friends among the younger set in town, and he taught several of us to dance to rock 'n' roll and swing. Thanks to John, I went off to college prepared to enjoy the dances at Virginia Tech and confident in my abilities as a dancer.

A few days after the enlisted men's dance, I was having a sandwich in Griffith's Lunchroom on Mason Avenue. The youth of the town often congregated there to put coins in the jukebox and tussle over which of the hit songs to play. I had no sooner seated myself in a booth with my grilled cheese sandwich and my French textbook than two of my officer friends, Lieutenant Martin and Captain Black, approached the booth where I was sitting alone and asked if they could join me. Of course I was delighted. Before long, one of them mentioned that they'd heard I had attended the enlisted men's dance. They explained that I had to choose whether to associate with the officers or enlisted personnel—the theory being that the officer class mixing with regular airmen broke down discipline. I chose not to choose. After all, I thought, military regulations did not apply to me.

Several years later, I was working in Washington, D.C. when my cousin, Andrew Hessman, introduced me to a college friend of his, John Chatel. We started dating. John and I had a good time together; in fact, I considered marrying him. John's father was from France. During the war, he had been liaison officer to the French general, Jacques-Philippe Leclerc. Now retired, he owned a real-estate business. Mr. Chatel, who was divorced, lived with his son in an old house in Georgetown. He went out of his way to show John and me a good time. Once, he gave John tickets to a Quatorze de Juillet dance sponsored by the French Embassy at one of the big hotels in D.C. Andrew, my sister Jane, and my brother Jerry went with John and me to the dinner dance.

Since the logistics of getting our group together took some time, we were late arriving at the dance. As we entered the ballroom, we felt fortunate to find one table right on the edge of the dance floor still unoccupied. Working our way around the outside of the crowd, we attained the table and hastened to seat ourselves. Our drinks had no sooner been served than the music stopped. A spotlight swung onto the double doors to the ballroom, and there in the doorway stood an elegant couple, the gentleman in a tuxedo and the lady in a gorgeous white designer gown. They were the evening's hosts, the popular French Ambassador Hervé Alphand and Madame Alphand, and as such, were announced with much fanfare. Under the spotlight, they slowly made their way across the ballroom, pausing to direct gracious nods to acquaintances. It was soon obvious that they were heading straight toward our table. Much to our alarm, we found ourselves caught within the scope of the floodlight. A couple of waiters rushed up and grabbed our glasses, whispering that we had to move. Other waiters scrambled to set up a table for us toward the back of the room. I felt the hot flush of embarrassment suffuse my face. What humiliation. We had come in late and unwittingly, like a bunch of heedless oafs, commandeered the table that had been reserved for the ambassador and his party!

Once the agitation of having made a faux pas abated, I had a wonderful evening. Unlike Americans, the Frenchmen were willing to ask a strange woman to dance. I danced with men of various ages, and once with a youngster who looked to be about twelve years old. The event was elegant, yet all so natural and relaxed. These French people knew how to have a good time.

Another evening, Mr. Chatel invited John and me to a dance at the Army & Navy Club. When the orchestra introduced a waltz, Mr. Chatel appeared before me and, with a slight bow, offered me his arm. He was very much the military man, with erect carriage and rather formal manners—and he was also an accomplished dancer. While we were whirling around the room, he expressed surprise that an American girl could waltz so beautifully. I had to smile to myself to think that I learned to waltz in the kitchen of the house on Fig Street and, indirectly, from an officer of the old Austro-Hungarian Empire. *One-two-three, one-two-three; step-up-down, step-up-down . . .*

A Cuisine

Mother learned to cook on the Eastern Shore. She did not know how to cook when she married because, when she was growing up, her mother kept a cook, and Mother had not been allowed in the kitchen when meals were being prepared. A year after her marriage, she found herself in Cape Charles with a two-month-old—me—and my hardworking father, who returned from work each day hungry for a hot meal. So she bought a cookbook, and then asked for the help of her next door neighbor, Mrs. Pruitt. With the aid of kindly neighbors and the cookbook, she became an excellent cook herself. Her new friends also counseled her on where to buy produce cheaply at the end of each season in order to can it for the coming winter.

Our cuisine was farm fare with lots of vegetables. We often had greens at dinner in the fall and winter. Turnip greens, mixed with mustard greens to add some bite, a slab of salt pork, or "fatback" as it was called, were cooked in a stockpot with a quart or more of water until very tender. They emerged from the big pot salty, greasy, satisfying—and delicious served up with fried oysters and corn pudding. I always enjoyed the "pot likker," as we referred to the liquid in which the greens had been cooked. Well-seasoned by the greens and the salt pork or a ham hock, it made a flavorful soup. On New Year's Day, one was well-advised to include ham hocks and turnip greens on the menu in order to insure good fortune for the coming year.

Sweet potatoes were a major crop on the Eastern Shore, so it wasn't surprising that sweet potatoes often appeared on the table in the form of a sweet potato casserole topped with marshmallows or pineapple, or both. There were also candied sweet potatoes, sweet potato biscuits, sweet potato rolls, sweet potato pie, sweet potato bread, sweet potato pudding, sweet potato . . . on and on. What a useful vegetable that was.

In those days, tomatoes were picked when red, not green, the way they are harvested today. All along the highway during tomato season, tomatoes rolled into the road from the overloaded trucks on their way to the packing sheds or Webster's Cannery. My father raised his own tomatoes, but, in season, bushels of tomatoes could be purchased for a nominal amount directly from the farms. Mother always put up many quarts of stewed tomatoes, and fried tomatoes were served as a side dish all summer long. We did not use green tomatoes for frying, as cooks did further south, but instead those that were red, yet still firm. They were sliced and covered with flour seasoned with salt and pepper, and fried a few minutes on both sides in a little oil or bacon grease. The cooking intensified their rich tomato taste, and though they sometimes fell apart, they had more flavor than fried green tomatoes could possibly have. My, but they were good!

Corn was almost as ubiquitous as greens, tomatoes, and sweet potatoes. What can equal the flavor of freshly picked corn that had been thrown into the pot just minutes from the garden and smothered in butter, salt, and pepper? So simple, so good. Corn pudding, corn fritters, corn and butterbeans, and plain corn shaved from the cob were frequent hosts at the dinner table.

Much of what was served was fried, but frying didn't seem to hurt us as none of us were fat, although Mother became a little plump later in life. On the coldest days of winter, we had fried cornmeal mush. Mother would cook the cornmeal on top of the stove. She then poured it into a bread pan and left it to congeal overnight in the refrigerator. In the morning, the resulting block of meal was turned out of the pan, sliced, rolled in salted flour, and fried in the big iron skillet. The fried slices formed a crust and were served with butter and syrup or honey. With a slice or two of bacon, sausage, or scrapple on the side, and a small dish of stewed fruit, it was a breakfast that could kept you warm inside all the way to school.

I learned to cook from my mother, much to my Yankee husband's dismay, until he developed a taste for such "exotic" dishes as turnip greens and grits. Years later, we were living in Richmond, Virginia when, one Sunday, our daughter Cynthia, who was a dancer with the Pittsburgh Ballet Company, made her weekly telephone call home. At that time, the director and most of the dancers of the Pittsburgh Ballet Company came from the Paris Opera Ballet. They had been touring the Northwest, the West, and the South of our country during the summer months. "Mamma, we're in Raleigh, North Carolina. This is our third day here, and at the hotel where we're staying, the food is just like the way you make it. And guess what? The French love it. Today at brunch, when I was at the table with dancers from Paris, everyone agreed when somebody said, 'Cette nourriture, cette mode de cuisiner—c'est bien une cuisine!' 'This food, this way of cooking—now, this is a cuisine!'"

Cottage-style Pure Oil station on Mason Avenue

CAPE CHARLES REVISITED

On a Monday afternoon in May of 2013, I drove from Richmond to the Eastern Shore with an artist friend, Nancy Blount. We came as members of a group of ten watercolor artists who were gathering in Cape Charles to paint scenes of the Eastern Shore. One of Nancy's friends had offered us the use of her condo at nearby Bay Creek Resort for our five-day stay—an offer we happily accepted.

I knew that I would be the only member of the group who had grown up in Cape Charles. What I hadn't expected were the constant flashbacks I experienced as we moved from one picturesque site to another. I had seldom visited Cape Charles since leaving in 1958, but on the few trips I'd made with my husband and children, I focused on their needs. Were they hungry? Were they getting sunburned? Were they bored? I'd had no opportunity to reflect on the past.

This time was different. This time, it was as if I were moving through the present and the past simultaneously. Knowing these recollections could mean nothing to the others, I kept them to myself.

The artists' group first met for dinner Monday evening at Kelley's Gingernut Irish Pub. The pub is housed in an old bank building on the corner of Mason Avenue and Pine Street. Another building, formerly the Farmer's and Merchant's Bank, stands on the opposite corner. It now contains the town's public library. Before entering the pub, I glanced at the Classical façade of the library.

In a flash, an almost-forgotten memory surfaced. After school in the mid-1950s, my sister, with her ponytail and her brown-and-white saddle shoes, would meet her teenage friends on Mason Avenue. Like birds perched on a clothesline, they sat along the ledge in front of the windows of the Farmer's and Merchant's Bank. Exchanging lively banter, they sipped the root beer floats they had just purchased from McMath's Drug Store, a few doors down the street.

The image quickly faded, and I entered the pub. We were ushered to the back of the restaurant to a room that was once the bank's vault. Dinner in a vault! Imagine that!

The next morning, Nancy and I drove along the professionally landscaped lanes of the Bay Creek Resort on our way to the Old Cape Charles Road. Azaleas in full bloom lined the drive beside the fairways of the golf course. Before us, a family of geese: momma, poppa, and three babies waddled down to the creek beside the golf links. The surroundings at Bay Creek were so beautiful that morning that I could happily have settled there to paint.

At Cape Charles Coffee House, we chatted with the owner over cups of rich coffee and a breakfast of pancakes and bacon. After breakfast, our group spent the morning painting some of the gardens behind houses near the beachfront. One of the organizers of our art tour, Shirley Hinkson from Richmond, invited us all to have lunch at her vacation house on Harbor Avenue overlooking the Bay near the remains of the pilings that had once supported the old Cape Charles Beach Casino.

After lunch, we piled into cars and headed to the little village of Oyster six miles north of Cape Charles. On the way out of town, we passed Rayfield's Pharmacy, where the ice plant once stood, and where my father used to bring our watermelons to be chilled in summer. On the Fourth of July, Daddy would cut open a big, sweet watermelon, its crisp pulp ice-plant-chilled to perfection.

In Oyster, we drove around the town. I missed the big barn-like structure that used to stand on the wharf. From it, seafood, mostly oysters, were loaded from the workboats onto trucks for shipping. It had once dominated the harbor as Oyster's center of commerce, but now it was gone!

We continued on to the home of a lady who lived in a house that overlooked a tranquil inlet across from Oyster and who, when we arrived, offered to let us use her front porch and yard as a place from which to paint.

When I was sixteen, my boyfriend Kenneth Doughty had lived on that inlet in a big white house. It had been brought to Oyster from Hog Island when the island started to wash away during a series of heavy storms. Kenneth used to do his homework by oil lamp, because there were not enough homes on that side of Oyster's harbor to make it profitable for the electric company to install service there.

I asked our hostess if she knew where the Doughty house was. "Yes," she said. "Actually, Kenneth was an older cousin of mine, but has passed away. His house was torn down years ago." Leaving her house unlocked so we could use her bathroom, she went back to her job as a Chesapeake Bay environmentalist.

That evening, the Stage Door Gallery, which now occupied the former Savage's Drug Store on Mason Avenue, hosted a reception for the artists. We walked into the spacious art gallery, and my eye immediately fell upon a ceramic bowl, on each side of which a fish was incised. The tails of the fish flipped up to form the bowl's handles. The vessel reminded me of the kind of pottery that had been produced along the Mediterranean coast in antiquity. (I have always been attracted to the Mediterranean. I blame Mrs. Vick, my high school Latin teacher; and Mrs. Chandler for introducing our class so enticingly to the *Iliad* and the *Odyssey*.) Before I had even accepted my first glass of wine, I bought the bowl, forcing our hostess to leave the guests and open the cash register.

The gallery had a good inventory of paintings, all effectively displayed and lighted. Wood carvings, prints, jewelry, and ceramics amply filled the shelves and display cases. It was reassuring to see business being conducted once more on Mason Avenue, but I couldn't help thinking, *Here is where the pharmacy section used to be. The soda fountain was over there. This corner must have been the storeroom where a congenial group of men raised their glasses of bourbon on Sunday afternoons. The lined notebook paper was kept here, next to Yeardley's English lavender soap. And didn't my paper smell wonderful, permeated with the sharply clean fragrance of lavender whenever I opened my binder?*

One of the reception's hosts offered to show us the Palace Theatre next to the Stage Door Gallery. He unlocked the door and we entered. It had been renovated, and was once more in use. It looked just the way it did in 1946, when I had embarrassed my family during a talent show by refusing to appear on stage after I had rehearsed my song for weeks and acquired a new dress for the occasion.

After the reception, we left to have dinner at Aqua, a large, modern restaurant with walls of windows that overlooked the Chesapeake Bay. It was located in Kings Creek Marina at the end of Fig Street. The marina had completely changed. Gone was the house from which the Richardson family supplied boaters with fuel, bait, and other items boaters and fishermen required. Mr. Spencer's repair shop and the old boat railway were gone. Now the marina appeared rather posh, with its 124-slip floating dock. It was neat, colorful, and attractive. But I missed the old marina's authentic Eastern Shore look, with its rambling weather-stained buildings supported above the water on wooden pilings.

We spent Wednesday painting on Onancock Creek, indisputably one of the most scenic places on the Eastern Shore.

The next day, our site was the town of Wachapreague, an oceanside port and a popular destination for serious fishermen. Wachapreague (\'*watch-uh-prig*\) is an Indian name meaning "Place on the Water."

It was a hot morning. Looking for the best available shade, we set up our easels in a pavilion at the location on which the majestic Hotel Wachapreague stood until it burned down in 1978. I started to outline the buildings across from the pavilion. I sketched in the road between the pavilion's park and the Island House Restaurant. Then a realization struck me. *That must be where we parked to gaze at the hotel through the windows of our old 1932 Pontiac.* I remembered "Rose Day."

When I was ten years old, our family attended Rose Day at the Gulf Stream Nursery near Wachapreague. Each year when the roses were in full bloom, the owners invited the public to visit the nursery. The Frenchmen who owned the nursery were on hand to answer questions and offer refreshments to their guests. I can still picture the look of pleasure on my father's face as he walked among the rosebushes, and wrote down the names of his favorites. He fell in love with two new varieties: "Mrs. Miniver," a fragrant, deep red rose; and "Peace," a pink-and-gold beauty that has become a favorite in American gardens. Both were bred in France and imported to the United States after the end of World War II. Daddy took a chance on these newcomers and bought one of each.

Since we were so close to Wachapreague, our parents decided to drive into the town to show their children the famous hotel. It was an imposing four-story frame building with wraparound balconies, and such a period piece that one could easily imagine ladies with pompadours and gentlemen in straw boaters, croquet mallets in hand, conversing on the lawn.

At lunchtime, we put our paints into our cars, walked across the street, and entered the air-conditioned comfort of the Island House. After a wonderful seafood meal (We really got our omega-3 that week!), refreshing glasses of iced tea, and a superb view overlooking the salt marsh, I was reluctant to return to the pavilion, which had now been invaded by the sun's rays. In spite of the heat, we stuck with the program.

In the evening, we dined on crab cakes at Sting-Ray's Restaurant on Route 13, near the entrance to the Bay Bridge Tunnel. Sting-Ray's is known for its excellent seafood and home-style cooking. It is part of the Cape Center gas station. When we walked in, I felt completely disoriented. I knew this place—at least, I had once.

Sting-Ray's had been called the Cape Center Restaurant when I lived on the Eastern Shore. Sometimes, teens from Cape Charles High School who had a driver's license or a friend with one used to go there for after school snacks. We sat beside the big glass windows that overlooked the gas pumps and filled up on soft drinks, sandwiches, and French fries. In those days, the Cape Center was spotlessly clean and flooded with natural light. With its red-and-white decor, the place had the look of a typical 1950s diner.

One afternoon when I was a junior in high school, my current boyfriend picked me up after school to drive us down the county to the Cape Center. Two girls from the senior class said that they would like to go there, too. We did not object, so they hopped into the car with us. The waitress came to the table to take our order. Out of consideration for my teenage beau, I just asked for a Coke and French fries. I felt mortified when the other girls ordered sandwiches, soft drinks, and dessert. I doubted that they could pay for it all. I was right. They expected to be treated. At the end of the meal, the waitress placed the bill on the table. No one made a move. I wanted to offer to contribute, but I knew that Kenneth would not like that, so he paid. Such were the mores of those times. The men always paid.

Today at Sting-Ray's, small tables are crammed together along the wall where the windows used to be, and the restaurant is full of assorted items for sale. One stands in line at a small counter to order his or her meal. The food, however, is very much admired, and that's what's most important. I know I had a delicious seafood platter.

My art group's last day on the Eastern Shore was dedicated to painting scenes in and around Cape Charles. I felt that I had been haunted enough by my former life, so Nancy and I spent the morning shopping in the small stores that line the main street. In midafternoon, we started back to Richmond, but not before we took a detour onto the road that leads to Pickett's Harbor. We had heard that the owners of Nottingham's Farm at Pickett's Harbor were selling freshly picked strawberries

At a crossroads, we encountered an SUV going in the opposite direction. We rolled down our window and asked for directions to Nottingham's Farm. The driver told us that she wasn't going that way but would lead us to the right turnoff. Instead, she stayed with us until we pulled up to Nottingham's packinghouse.

Nancy bought a flat containing eight quarts of bright red, flawless strawberries. I bought a flat to distribute to some of my real estate clients. Our guide decided that, since she was there, she would buy strawberries to give to her children's teachers. All the way back to Richmond, the fragrance of sun-warmed strawberries filled the cab of Nancy's SUV.

Afterword: A Brief History of Cape Charles

When I was a child, the "holy trinity" that sustained the economy of the Eastern Shore of Virginia was comprised of agriculture, the seafood industry, and the Pennsylvania Railroad. Ever since America's Colonial days, farming has been the major economic driver on the Eastern Shore. Commerce depended on the success of the farm families and the seafood industry. For two centuries, most of the agricultural and seafood harvests were sent to market by water; either to the port of Baltimore, or through Norfolk. In the 1880s, a new railroad and ferry complex opened, providing farmers with a faster way to ship their goods to the big produce markets in Philadelphia and New York. The headquarters for the railroad was located in Cape Charles, and new people, many from the North, were sent to Cape Charles to oversee the operations of the railroad and the ferries that connected the Eastern Shore to Norfolk and Little Creek, Virginia.

There was naturally some antipathy toward the newcomers on the part of those whose ancestors had worked the fertile land for centuries, and whose culture reflected Southern rural values with a social hierarchy that, broadly speaking, placed the landowners at the top of the social scale, those in the seafood industry beneath them, and those who provided the farm labor at the bottom. The educated people who moved in from the industrial North brought new ideas, and Jews and Catholics appeared among the population of the town. The new arrivals did not fit into the established order. The county families and the newcomers, however, needed each other. Farmers relied on the railroad to get their crops to market, and the town depended on the local people to supply teachers, rail and ferry workers, restaurants, and retail stores. Some county families moved to Cape Charles to avail themselves of the comforts that a well-planned community could provide. The town grew and prospered.

Although it was located at the far end of the Delmarva Peninsula, Cape Charles soon became the commercial hub for Northampton and Accomack counties. The largest department store in the counties, Wilson's Department Store, attracted customers from all over the countryside. Many farm families were drawn into the civic life of Cape Charles. They joined the Rotary Club, the Woman's Club, or the Municipal Library. Some county children attended school in Cape Charles; others participated in talent competitions and fashion shows held at the Palace Theatre. Children from the town and country made friends with each other. The culture in Cape Charles became a blend of Southern gentility and Northern energy.

The entry of the United States into the Second World War in 1941 created a demand by the military for the shipment of food, equipment, and personnel. This gave a financial boost to the farmers and towns along the rail line, especially to Cape Charles, with its fleet of tugs, barges, and ferries—and its trains. Businesses on Mason Avenue prospered. The farmers had money to spend, and travelers using the trains and ferries patronized the restaurants and shops. Servicemen taking the "Furlough Specials" that carried soldiers and sailors between the northern cities and the military bases in the South crowded into the restaurants for meals that were more appetizing than the dried-out food served on the troop trains.

After the war, one by one, like pieces being pulled from its pile in a game of pick-up-sticks, the drivers of the economy in Cape Charles were withdrawn. The railroad experienced a decline in business, as the increased use of refrigerated trucks gave the farmers the flexibility to send their produce to markets as far away as Canada, or wherever they could command the best prices. The demand for the transport of wartime materials and military personnel ended. The Pennsylvania Railroad retired one of its tracks and reduced its service.

In 1950, in order to shorten the Chesapeake Bay crossing, the fleet of ferries that operated between Cape Charles and Norfolk or Little Creek, except the steamer *Elisha Lee*, was moved to a new terminal at Kiptopeke Beach, eight miles south of town. Route 13, the main road that served the Delmarva Peninsula, had been shifted to bypass Cape Charles when it was then rerouted to carry the traffic to Kiptopeke Ferry Terminal.

In April of 1953, without warning and much to the sorrow of the citizenry, the *Elisha Lee* failed a Coast Guard inspection and was placed in dry dock in Hampton Roads. Townspeople formed committees to fight to retain the ferry; the Cape Charles Chamber of Commerce petitioned to keep a ferry in Cape Charles; the Eastern Shore Civic Association sought donations to enable it to purchase a replacement vessel. From the spring of 1953 through June of 1954, a succession of lawsuits was brought against the ferry's owner, the Pennsylvania Railroad. After much litigation, the Interstate Commerce Commission ruled that lack of profitability justified shutting down the rail and ferry service.

In 1952 and 1953, Cape Charles bravely hosted the Miss Virginia contest. The fanfare of a parade and the beauty contest at the Palace Theatre injected a note of excitement into the community, but by then, the future looked uncertain. What industry could possibly replace the once-powerful railroad? What jobs would be eliminated? Whose salaries reduced?

Although speculations about the future were worrisome, life for the next few years continued as usual in Cape Charles. In May of 1953 and 1954, the town celebrated Armed Forces Day. Sponsored by Cape Charles Air Force Station (formerly called Fort Custis), the program provided a full day of activities. A parade of floats accompanied by marching bands from Norfolk Naval Base and Langley Air Force Base formed on Fig Street and continued down Mason Avenue to Bay Avenue. A few short speeches honoring our military were delivered at the boardwalk pavilion, followed by a flyover. Visiting ships filled the harbor. In the afternoon, an archery contest and a baseball game took place at nearby Patton Field. The Air Force Station held an open house, and in the evening, there was a dance at the American Legion Hall.

By the late 1950s, most of the town families were trying to survive with less income. In 1959, the railroad station was torn down. All remaining evidence of the town's original reason for existing vanished when, at the request of Cape Charles City Council, the railroad shops and roundhouse were demolished in 1960. One by one, the stores began to close, until Mason Avenue became a street of boarded-up buildings. Many townspeople with marketable skills—those who were still young enough to be employed elsewhere—moved away, as did some of the merchants.

The town of Cape Charles remained on the edge of the Bay like a discarded seashell lying on the beach. Several decades of decline had changed the bustling community into a sleepy backwater. But lack of progress preserved the charm of its residential section, and left the Cape Charles Historic District ripe for renewal.

Since then, like Rip Van Winkle rising from a long slumber, the town of Cape Charles has experienced a new awakening. Developers, realizing the potential for a viable resort in the area and the availability of large tracts of land, established Bay Creek Resort, a planned community of homes built around an Arnold Palmer Signature Golf Course, in 1993. The promotion of Bay Creek Resort drew attention not only to the resort but to the historic district of Cape Charles. Attracted by the town's old homes and lovely bayside location, buyers from outside the Eastern Shore bought and renovated many of the dilapidated houses in the historic district, which they use as vacation homes or rent to tourists.

In 2013, Home and Garden Television—HGTV—filmed an episode for the series "Beachfront Bargain Hunt," in Cape Charles. The episode featured a couple visiting Cape Charles to look for a beach house they could buy at an affordable price, and on top of attracting a nationwide audience, encouraged other potential homebuyers to consider investing in Cape Charles.

A new business, the Cape Charles Yacht Center, opened in July of 2014. Making use of the old ferry harbor with its eighteen-foot-deep channel, the new yacht center now provides anchorage and services to oceangoing superyachts as they travel from New England to Florida and back.

With a population of around a thousand permanent citizens, Cape Charles may be small, but it is home to several excellent restaurants. A lively arts program of plays, music, and dance is centered in the restored Palace Theatre. The Tall Ships Festival in June attracts visitors from distant locations to cruise in the tall ships, listen to pirate tales, and enjoy music. An annual progressive dinner, at which the public can view the Christmas decorations in several of the town's homes, provides a midwinter activity, as does the Dropping of the Crab Pot on New Years Eve. In the latter case, a six-by-six-foot box of wire fencing covered with Christmas lights is decorated with a metal crab. The crab pot is then lifted ninety feet into the air, and the Volunteer Fire Department serves hot cider and hot chocolate as citizens wait for the crab pot to drop.

Another highlight of the holiday season, the Epiphany Party, is traditionally held in the firehouse on the first Saturday after Epiphany. Sponsors of the party invite anyone who would like to attend to bring their "least favorite Christmas present" to be auctioned off. Proceeds from the auction help finance a civic need. In 2013, the Epiphany Party raised $4,279 for the town's library, and in 2015, the auction realized around $5,500 to repair the municipal playground.

Since 1991, the same two pink garden flamingos have appeared on the block at each auction. They always bring the highest bid of the evening, and year after year, the bid increases. In 2015, they were knocked down at over $750. What will they bring next year?

Cape Charles continues to grow and prosper. Today, this Rip Van Winkle of a town is wide awake!

ACKNOWLEDGEMENTS

Thank you to all who helped make this book possible. A big thank-you to Roberta Romeo, proprietor of the Cape Charles Coffee House, who saw a need for an account of the days when the Pennsylvania Railroad drove the local economy. It was she who encouraged me to publish my memoir. Thanks to Bill Neville for making the trip from Princess Anne, Maryland to open the archives at the Cape Charles Historical Society and Museum for my use; for accompanying me to some ancient cemeteries; for always being available to answer my questions; and for sharing his memories with me. Marion Narr, president of the Cape Charles Historical Society, sent a copy of an old ferry schedule that clearly showed that the trip from Cape Charles to Norfolk took two hours and fifty minutes in the 1940s. Virginia Savage of the Historical Society sent me a copy of Miss Kate Savage's 1929 poem "The Private in the Ranks." Thank you, Virginia and Marion.

My appreciation goes to the Writers' Critique group at the Lifelong Learning Institute of Chesterfield County, who under the guidance of Dorothy Moses forced me to stick to my writing schedule. Thanks to the Virginia Library for providing microfilm of old copies of the *Northampton Times*, *Eastern Shore News* and the *Peninsula Enterprise* newspapers, invaluable sources for checking the accuracy of my memories.

Thank you to George Ronald Ferguson, Donna Edgerton,

Carol Drennen Rush, and J. Donald Etz for sharing their family photographs containing scenes from which the illustrator, Hugh Harris, drew to portray sites in Cape Charles as they were in the 1940s. Thanks to Carol Drennen Rush for giving me a copy of her old map of Cape Charles. John and Mary Harlow, thank you for sending me the current Cape Charles phone book. A tribute to my husband, George Parsons, who never showed that he was tired of hearing my stories about Cape Charles, and who drove me from Richmond to the Eastern Shore many times. My son-in-law, David Woodmansee, was the only person, with the exception of my publisher, to have read my entire manuscript. Thanks for telling me that you liked my stories. To Richmond author Kathleen Reid: Thanks for your smart ideas and for encouraging me to join James River Writers.

I am grateful to Robert Pruett, publisher of Pleasant Living Books, for accepting my manuscript and for guiding me through publication. Thanks to Erin Harpst for editing *Portrait of a Town* with insight, great care, and professionalism. Tom Trenz, designer, you are a pleasure to work with; and Tim Hagood, publicist, thanks for being available to answer my questions about the publishing process.

My appreciation goes to Dorie Southern for publishing an article about the pending book in the *Cape Charles Wave*. Thank you, Niki Sabbath, for your article promoting *Portrait of a Town* in the Oxford Observer.

To Donna and Greg Kohler of the Fig Street Inn: Thank you for making me comfortable during my stay with you and sending me on my information gathering forays fortified by an excellent breakfast.

About the Author

Born in Pittsburgh, Pennsylvania, Patricia Joyce Parsons moved to Cape Charles, Virginia as an infant when her father's employment with the Pennsylvania Railroad transferred the family to the Eastern Shore of Virginia. Growing up in Cape Charles, Pat experienced the carefree lifestyle of a small town juxtaposed against the hustle and bustle of wartime efforts flowing in and out of the Chesapeake Bay and the nearby Norfolk naval shipyards. Like many of her contemporaries, Pat left Cape Charles as the town began to dwindle in the post-war period. She attended Radford University, and subsequently, found employment in Washington, D.C. at the Securities and Exchange Commission and the Air Transport Association. In 1963, Pat married Boston born lawyer, George Parsons, and together they moved to Richmond, Virginia as their family began to grow and the desire for a less complicated life began to emerge. In Richmond, Pat raised five children and has been a real estate agent for over twenty-six years. In her spare time, she has volunteered as a French teacher for the Lifelong Learning Institute of Chesterfield County and served on the boards of the Oxford Civic Association and the Richmond Chapter of the National Society of Arts and Letters.

Pat has always had an interest in writing. She was published in the *Radford Review* and periodically contributes to civic publications, but somehow, the business of raising a large family left little time to write. She considers herself an accidental author. Beginning with a memoir for her family (which she had no intention of publishing), Pat stumbled across the idea for her first published book, *Portrait of a Town*. In returning to her hometown to research her original memoir, Pat realized, through conversations with current residents, that she possessed a historical memory of Cape Charles that had never been published. She decided to use her vivid memories to bring the town and era of her childhood to life through a colorful collection of vignettes depicting daily life from a unique perspective.

Pat plans to continue her writing in the same vain as *Portrait of a Town*. She feels she has found her niche with a charming, personal, yet historically-based style.

About the Illustrator

Hugh Harris is a Richmond, Virginia artist, and a retired pastor, who has lived in several Chesapeake Bay communities and painted Bay subjects over many years. He is also an author, having published three novels in his Dinkel Island Series that is set in Virginia's Northern Neck region of the Chesapeake Bay.